Rachel Conrad Wahlberg

Jesus According to a Woman

[Revised and Enlarged edition]

PAULIST PRESS
New York/Mahwah

The Publisher gratefully acknowledges the following:
Selections from the poem "The Wit and Wisdom of Midwives," page 33 of
Eve and After: Old Testament Women in Portrait, by Thomas John Carlisle,
copyright 1984 by Wm. B. Eerdmans Publishing Co., are used by permission.

Library of Congress
Catalog Card Number: 74-27461

ISBN: 0-8091-1861-0

Published by Paulist Press
997 Macarthur Boulevard
Mahwah, N.J. 07430

Printed and bound in the
United States of America

CONTENTS

INTRODUCTION

In the period of ten years since I wrote this book, a great deal of change has taken place. Today there is a term, "Christian feminist" or "Christian feminism," with which I can identify, a term unknown in the 1960s and 1970s. I felt when I was writing these essays that I was somewhat alone in my perceptions. At some level I was trying to integrate the secular women's movement with what I knew to be the reality, the core, the kernel of Christianity—that women are indeed made in God's image, and that there is neither Jew nor Greek, neither slave nor free, neither male nor female, that we are all one in Christ (Gen. 1:27; Gal. 3:28).

Today many of us recognize that biblical interpretation and preaching has been filtered through the biases, the social conditioning and cultural assumptions of the persons expressing the views. We acknowledge that we have received messages about our faith, Scripture and Christian history from those who are and were integrated into a patriarchal system. Indeed, all biblical interpretation is skewed by a point of view, an androcentric bias, by the patriarchal underpinnings and sociological assumptions of ancient Graeco-Roman culture— or the Western white male intellectual system of the more recent past.

It was this mind-set that I struggled with, fighting against the negative, stereotypical interpretations of Scripture that related to women.

But as I reflect on the past, I see that in my own life there were several stimulants which led to the creation of *Jesus According to a Woman* and *Jesus and the Freed Woman*. In addition to coming from a Germanic background, which encouraged independent thinking, college debating, writing and speaking, in the late 1960s and early 1970s I was a participant in a Protestant-Catholic dialogue group in Austin, Texas.

This dialogue group was a shaping force in my life as I began to see that all of us—Catholic sisters, Episcopal professor, Baptists, Presbyterians (including Dr. Rachel Henderlite, seminary professor and first woman ordained by the southern Presbyterian church), Lutherans, homemakers and professionals—had essentially the same beliefs. And I saw that as women we had all been marginalized and discriminated against in our own churches. I began to see a convergence among us as Christians, as well as the fact that we women could explore Scripture and theology for ourselves without guidance from male "authorities."

During the 1960s for eight years I had taught an adult class in my own church, exploring almost the entire New Testament, with fifteen to twenty-five other daring, creative adults. We shared our insights, provoking each other to many lively discussions. We used our imaginations to interpret, share how we felt about certain passages, and discover meanings and insights we had never thought of before. Not only did we acknowledge the woman-demeaning nature of much criticism, but we discovered again and again exciting, affirming ways to look at certain Gospel stories. And we found support in Krister Stendhal's *The Bible and the Role of Women* (Fortress Press, 1966) and other scholars' writings, concerning what was appropriate in the first century and what is acceptable in the twentieth.

Without this intensive period of research, study and lively exchange, I would not have had the grounding and the common understanding from ordinary Christians, which prepared me to write these essays about Jesus and women.

Another shaping force was the writing I was doing for various church magazines—*The Lutheran, Christian Century,*

Presbyterian Life (and later *A.D.*), Methodist *Together* (and later *Today*), *Theology Today, New Catholic World,* etc.

One writing project—some parable studies—for a national church women's organization directly led to my frame of mind for *Jesus According to a Woman.*

My instructions were to select five parables which would be most meaningful to women. The story of the widow who pestered the judge popped into mind. What an activist, I thought. She really got results because she nagged the judge until he gave her justice. The parable about yeast and bread was another that women could identify with. Thinking of my own breadmaking and what yeast does to the other ingredients, I felt that Christians should be just such a disturbing, disruptive, generating, explosive influence. And so on.

Unknown to me the officers overseeing this project submitted my writings to a New Testament professor in an eastern seminary. The professor objected that I had given some original interpretations to these parables which were not in line with traditional interpretations. According to him, one must not offer interpretations which have not been traditionally offered. The church women's group, to their credit, declined to "water down" or explain away my interpretation of the five parables.

As the modern women's movement came on the scene, I began to notice other insights in Scripture that were not perceived or mentioned in the average Sunday morning sermon or Bible study. It occurred to me that Jesus in his relationships with women always treated women with intimacy, high regard and naturalness. I began to notice that the church has emphasized negative examples and passages from the Bible concerning women, rather than positive examples which do exist. Not only was the Eve story exaggerated far out of proportion in order to criticize women, but I began to see that Eve was a strong, decisive person (even though mistaken) and that

Adam was weak, easily influenced, and a coward (See my article, "Much Ado About Eve," *Presbyterian Life,* March 15, 1972.) Disobedient Israel (Gomer) was a whoring wife; her husband (Hosea) was a god-figure. Sermons were preached often on Paul's put-down passages about women with the overtones of paternalism and rejection of sex. The traditional wedding service was built around these passages: "Wives, be subject to your husbands as to the Lord." (How could marriage be a partnership if one person is subject and one person is Lord?) "Husbands, love your wives as your own body." (This one always rankled; who wants to be loved merely as a body? Marriage is a relationship between two persons — not a *person* and a *body.*)

Not only have women heard negative ideas about themselves in Bible study, marriage services, and sermons, but almost no churches had visible women ministers. Those Protestant churches who ordained women rarely found places for them in congregations except as assistants or youth directors or in small rural parishes.

Aside from the fact that few women looked to the church for employment or careers, women were internalizing certain ideas about themselves. From girlhood on, women were absorbing and reinforcing negative ideas and images from their received concepts of Christianity:

- women are Eves, temptresses;
- women are subordinate to males at all levels;
- women are not to speak in church, and in some churches they are not to teach adults;
- women were not counted — as in the feeding of the five thousand *men,* "not counting women and children";
- stories which dramatized evil women were commonly cited and elaborated in curriculum materials;

- women had no models in theology or in Bible study other than Eve and Mary;
- to be a deaconess or sister, a woman must give up normal sex, marriage, children and independence;
- women were put down in numerous passages from Paulinist writers: "It is better not to touch a woman"; "Let the women keep quiet; if they want to know anything, let them ask their husbands at home"; "Women will be saved through childbirth";
- women followers of Jesus were not taken seriously as disciples;
- Jewish women were unclean during their periods and after childbirth.

In 1971 *Catholic World* published Leonard Swidler's "Jesus Was a Feminist." At that time I had a writing folder on my desk labeled "Jesus Was a Woman's Liberationist." Not only were women writing secular books about discrimination against women in secular life, but people began to discuss sexism in religion. Georgia Harkness, Mary Daly, Rosemary Radford Ruether, Letty Russell, Virginia Ramey Mollencott, Elisabeth Schussler Fiorenza and others were zeroing in on the second-class position women have and have had historically in Christendom. Women's commissions and consulting committees were formed in most Protestant churches. Catholic women in religious orders began speaking out for more freedom of choice, for the right to determine their own rules and to define their own Christian mission.

As a teacher and lecturer on the subject of "The Changing Image of Women in Church and Society," I began to take notes on how Jesus related to women. As I studied various passages, I began to perceive a model in Jesus for full adult relationships. I encouraged women in discussion groups to speak out about what had been lurking in their minds about Jesus. I asked them how they felt about certain passages and stories. One woman said, "I always hated the story of Mary and Martha. Not only was I a Martha in my style of life, but my *name* is Martha. I squirmed every time I heard that story." She had not worked it out in her own mind why she hated it. She just felt miserable.

Other women mentioned how important to them was the story of the woman "caught" in adultery, because Jesus blamed the men and did not condemn the woman. Others objected vocally to the way Jesus' mother Mary has been presented throughout Christian history—as sexless, as only a virgin or a mother, as obedient when she was obviously coerced and had no freedom of choice.

As a teacher of adults in Christian education classes, I observed that in Bible commentaries, whenever incidents involving Jesus and a woman were discussed, some side issue would dominate the exegesis or exposition. In considering the woman at the well, the writer would go off into digressions about the differences between the Samaritans and the Jews and about the history of Jacob's well, and minimize the woman's response and actions. Sermons as well seemed generally evasive about women's assertive actions. On Easter Sunday when women are noticed for coming to the empty tomb and for seeing the risen Lord, I noticed that the women were never credited for what in fact they *did*—going and telling, spreading the news, witnessing.

Christianity has not seen, as Swidler pointed out, that the woman sweeping for the lost coin is a God figure seeking the lost. Instead, thousands of sermons are preached on the prodigal son to make the same point. And the uppity woman (with whom I identify intensely) who argues with Jesus about the crumbs is not perceived as a daring, aggressive person and debater.

And so these stories came about.

Both women and men are beginning to see that Jesus had a far more perceptive mind than we had given him credit for. Incredibly, however, we cannot understand *his* perceptions until our own minds open to see things in a new light. What he did has not changed. The fact is that he alone among the people in the New Testament did not accept a first-century mold for women. He alone treated women as whole persons. Whereas Paul and Peter penned extremely repressive passages about women, today's doctrinal studies in many constituencies of Christendom are boldly saying that those passages were typical of first-century culture and religion but are not normative for all time.

Perceptions must change first—and this is happening. Then attitudes change, and this is happening. Then actions begin to change. And this too is beginning to happen.

I see a shift in consciousness resulting in affirmative action in many areas of church and society.

In general there are several trends. First there is an attempt to sex-integrate the structures of church and society. Not only are women in unprecedented numbers entering law, politics, and many professions regarded as reserved for men, but a drastic concept change is taking place in many of the major church bodies. The women's movement has taken hold in *both* society and church, stimulating a changed mind-set, an upheaval in our approach to equality, to ministry, and to a more equal representation of women and men at all levels.

During the 1970s and 1980s there has been a dramatic increase in the proportion of women attending theological seminaries. Two Lutheran bodies made decisions to ordain women. The Episcopal church, after a dramatic challenge by a small group of women who were ordained priests in an unauthorized service, followed by a controversial period, also agreed to allow women to become priests. Among Methodists several women have been elected as bishops. And even some

Southern Baptist congregations have ordained a few women although the church itself takes an official stand against the principle of ordination of women.

Among Catholics, women continued to reflect on Vatican II and its meaning for their lives and ministry. Not only did women religious exchange their habits for secular dress, but many moved out into the secular communities to serve in new ways. In the late 1970s women's coalitions began to form to promote more independence, to recognize and discuss oppressive treatment, and to push for women's ordination to the priesthood. The Women's Ordination Conference has blossomed, developing an organization and networking newsletter, and claiming several thousand women who feel called to become priests.

Both in society and church, women are beginning to move out of men's shadows where they have usually done work for a male superior, and are asking for job advancement opportunities for themselves. Social conditioning of girls and women is beginning to change. Women's groups are insisting that girls not be image-boxed in textbooks and career-planning, that the real potential girls start out with should not be squelched by social pressure and school counseling into limited activities and low-talent jobs—the same low expectation treatment which minorities have complained about.

There is also a move to liberate theology from some of its patriarchal assumptions and traditions. Theologians such as Fiorenza and Trible and Ruether are pointing out how male-oriented bias has served to gloss over, ignore, or belittle the contributions of women in very critical ways.

For example, in an essay in *The Liberating Word* (Westminister, 1976, edited by Letty Russell, pp. 49ff.), Fiorenza describes Miriam as a co-equal of Moses and Aaron, but notes that she is treated as a rebellious daughter. Modern commentators on the story of her and Aaron's rebellion against Moses "cannot conceive of Miriam as an independent leader in Israel, but only as the jealous and rebellious sister of Moses with whom Yahweh deals as a patriarchal father would handle his uppity daughter."

Likewise, the women around Jesus who were the closest to him, who were privileged to be his first messengers (see last chapter of this book, "Jesus and the Women Preachers"), have been belittled and in some cases written out of the gospel story. Even though Luke, for example, relates the story of the women at the tomb and their subsequent telling of their experience to "all the rest," he diminishes it by saying the words "seemed to them an idle tale, and they did not believe them" (Lk. 24:12). He further excludes the witness of the women in the statement (24:34) that "the Lord is risen and has appeared to Simon!" For Paul's glaring omission of the resurrection appearance to the women, see the chapter, "Jesus and the Women Preachers."

However, both Mark and John show the women around Jesus as true disciples, with Martha, Mary of Magdala, and Mary of Bethany holding prominent places.

Yet Fiorenza argues that the trend toward patriarchy in the early Church may have been a reaction to the equal discipleship of women and men, slaves and masters, Jews and Greeks, etc. This co-equal discipleship created tension and reaction from the social-political environment. Thus the household rules of Colossians, Timothy, Titus and Peter may be a patterning of the Church after the social constructs of the later first and early second century....

Many questions remain for Christian feminists—and the Church. While we cannot eliminate the male-oriented, male-dominated character of Scripture, can we find sufficient women-affirming principles and interpretations to reestablish women and cast them in a more central position in biblical studies, in Church history and in today's ecclesiastical structures?

What does it mean that both woman and man are made in

God's image? What does it mean that in Christ there is neither Jew nor Greek, neither slave nor free, neither male nor female? How significant is it that Jesus was male? Was his prime importance humanness rather than maleness?

Sin must be defined from the woman's point of view as well as the man's. To identify sin with pride, lust and aggressiveness, women writers are suggesting, is to indicate what *men* feel guilty about, not women. Women, like blacks, have been cautioned to hold back, be subject, suffer quietly in this world, do menial jobs. Thus, women's sin is to be self-denying, self-demeaning, reluctant to admit strength and God-given creativity and potential.

To redefine sin also calls for a reconsideration of the fall and its sexual guilt/sin simplifications. Church teaching and preaching must reflect Jesus' affirmation of women, deliberately rejecting the historic association of women with sexual sin which has resulted in anti-women interpretations in the past. To balance nineteen centuries of Christian dogma interpreted from the male point of view, women writers, professors and theologians are needed to balance out negative attitudes concerning women which pervade major Christian thinkers from Paul and Augustine to the present.

Yet the undervaluing of what women do, and what women said and accomplished as disciples of Jesus and in the early Church, continues. What women did was much more dramatic and vital than we have realized. It has been easy to ignore their importance and to regard women as on the edges of the real action, rather than at the vital center participating equally.

Jean Baker Miller says that in a general way, "male society recognizes as activity only what men do" and most "so-called women's work is not recognized as real activity." Especially if women are helping others rather than helping themselves, "this is seen as *not doing anything" (Toward a New Psychology of Women,* p. 52).

- Consider the silly, emotional act of the woman at Simon's who anointed Jesus. What she did was not regarded as important; she was an intrusion, an embarrassment. Yet her assertive act was a dramatic event in Jesus' life—far more important than the critical men gathered at Simon's could see—or even those Gospel writers who recorded it.
- Consider Mary Magdalene's conversation with the resurrected Lord. Consider that the women were the first to tell the resurrection news, the first preachers of that Easter day.
- Consider the woman at the well carrying on a theological discussion with Jesus…and Mary and Martha in conflict over who gets the privilege of sharing Jesus' conversation and company.
- Consider the woman who argues back when Jesus says that he is sent to the house of David. She is sharp—even the dogs, she points out, have rights to the crumbs under the master's table. And Jesus is forced to pause and reflect on her words.
- And the woman as a God figure seeking the lost coin—just as the shepherd looked for a lost sheep and a father his lost child.

Were these women *not doing anything?*

Or is there dynamic power in the acts and messages we receive from the women in these stories?

Now we know. These women were integral to the story and actions of Jesus and the early Church.

I believe it is the image of whole men and women living the precepts of the Gospel that is the greatest need of the church today. The women's movement, by inspiring new self-awareness among persons of both sexes and by encouraging such explorations as I offer in this book, is contributing to a fuller, richer Christianity.

If we are not all liberated in Christ, then no one is liberated. It is imperative that all free-spirited women and men insist that the church carry out its true freedom in the Gospel by dispelling at all levels—and in all its segments, doctrine, hierarchies, interpretation and preaching—any vestiges of discrimination against any group of people.

The church can only benefit if full ability, insight and performance are expected from 100% of its members, not just the male 45%. The goal of Christians is to be neither Greek nor Jew, neither slave nor free, neither male nor female, but full persons doing the work of Jesus Christ.

JESUS AND THE
UPPITY WOMAN

Mark 7:24-30; Matthew 15:21-28

Because of the feminist movement, many attitudes, incidents and stories in Scripture are being examined today with fresh insight. Traditionally, the woman-affirming implications of some passages have gone unrecognized. For example, Matthew and Mark tell a great story about a woman who did not know her place.

The story is about an uppity woman.* She felt that she could relate to the popular healer Jesus on a one-to-one basis. She could say what was on her mind. She did the unthinkable—she talked back to Jesus. The story has always been there; now we see the woman's daring and self-assertion.

First of all she came from Tyre and Sidon, a Canaanite woman. In the popular prejudice of the day she was a second-rate person to the Jews—including Jesus himself. And she was a woman.

Her purpose is simple. She cries out, "Have mercy, O Lord, Son of David; my daughter is severely possessed by a demon."

The woman had a just cause. In the first century, possession by a demon was an accepted label for conditions now known as epilepsy or mental sickness. Only a person closely

---

*Note the way certain words are used to put down women: "uppity," "pushy," "strident," "bossy." If a man has these characteristics, he is bold, confident, courageous, dynamic. "Uppity" here is used in a tongue-in-cheek way. This woman is bold, confident, courageous, dynamic, self-assertive.

involved with a sick child could know the trauma, the anguish, the need. It gave her the selfless courage to seek out Jesus.

At first, Matthew reports, Jesus is cool toward the woman. He does not say a word. To us this reaction seems out of character for a person who went about doing good, ministering to the needs of people.

Not only did Jesus react coolly, but his disciples attempted to constrain him by giving him negative advice: "Send her away, for she is crying after us."

The disciples meant to make it easy for Jesus but lacked discrimination as to what was significant. When Jesus does speak to the woman he sounds defensive: "I was sent only to the lost sheep of the house of Israel."

One must try to imagine Jesus' tone. Is he peevish? Angry? Torn with compassion but not wanting to give in to the woman's demand? You are not our kind, he implies. I am to minister to my people—not to people like you. Or, is Jesus defending himself, apologizing for his narrow definition of himself as a leader only of Jews?

Many Bible scholars accept the idea that there was a time in his ministry when Jesus did feel his mission was only to the Jews. Although his mission was later expanded to include all people, no one can say with accuracy just when such expansion occurred in the mind of Jesus. Some interpreters think that Jesus did not understand himself totally and that it took the later interpretation of Paul to make the Gospel inclusive of Gentile as well as Jew.

Modern Christians, seeing Jesus from the perspective of centuries, find it difficult to understand the limited concept Jesus is expressing in this story. *Sent only to the Jews?*

Although Paul said "there is neither Jew nor Greek, neither slave nor free, neither male nor female," we forget that in the first century there truly *were* Jew and Greek, slave and free, male and female. These were three givens, accepted divisions or barriers of the day. Thus Jesus did see the woman in this incident as outside the "house of Israel."

The undaunted woman uses her first option. She kneels before Jesus and appeals to his compassion: "Lord help me."

That appeal should melt the hardest of persons—and certainly the compassionate Jesus. But oddly enough, he continues to argue with her in a defensive, elitist, Jew-oriented way: "It is not fair to take the children's bread and throw it to the dogs."

The appeal had not worked. How could he say such a harsh thing if he were truly a healer who cared about people? There is no way his argument does not come out as harsh—the Jews are the "children"; her people are the "dogs." It is unkind, a put-down.

We have believed that Jesus could not speak unkindly, that he was not a victim of the prejudices of his own Jewish home and community. Obviously if non-Jews were looked down upon in the Jewish community, Mary and Joseph and Jesus would have absorbed the prejudice. We say glibly that Jesus was *human*, but whenever he displays a *humanly-conditioned prejudice,* we feel that we must deny it. He had to be godly at all points—*our* concept of godly—not a human being with prejudices and preconceived notions about superiority, not really a man of his times.

(In general, the unkindness of his put-down to the Canaanite woman has been blocked out through centuries of interpretation. Was it perhaps because male interpreters could not identify with the insulted woman, or because Jesus was actually taking a hard line, a non-compassionate line against this woman which must be explained away? Traditional interpreters have suggested that he was testing her faith, an explanation easy to read into a story if one knows the ending is upbeat and if one cannot grant simple human prejudice to Jesus.)

Existentially, then—as a man and a woman communicating at that moment—the saying was harsh and unfeeling. It chokes in the throat of any woman reader who identifies with another woman asking help for a child.

Quickly now the woman moves to her second option. She was not only resourceful, she was an excellent debater. She was, in a word, magnificent in her retort. She gets uppity.

"Yes, Lord, yet even the dogs eat crumbs that fall from their master's table."

We do not know *her* tone either. It could have been humble or arrogant or desperate. No matter. The argument was forceful and strong. She makes a valid point. Can Jesus deny it? The Jews may be the superior race in these parts but even foreign dogs have rights. And wasn't she asking for crumbs?

Jesus capitulates. He says, according to Matthew, "O woman, great is your faith." And her daughter is healed. But Mark—who is credited with the earlier account—is probably more accurate. "For this saying you may go your way; the demon has left your daughter." *For this saying.*

Obviously a story which is recorded some decades after it happens cannot perfectly record the nuances of tone or the exact phrasing of a sentence, even a climactic one. "For this saying" indicates that Jesus responded specifically to her argument—it was not just her faith that impressed him. It was her bright answer, her forceful and intelligent answer. *For this saying your daughter is healed.*

Jesus endorses the very spirit of the woman, her indomitable snappy spirit. Her faith, we remember, was indicated in her first appeal for help, and Jesus had been cool to that. But he became aware of her as a person, and responded as the person of stature he was.

There are two implications here for the modern Bible interpreter. First, this woman did not fit the subordinate mold for women in patriarchal society. She was so absorbed in the tragedy of her child that she had the selfless courage, the aggressiveness to seek out the popular Jesus.

Obviously the woman has nothing to lose in this story except Jesus' attention—and her hope for help. So why not challenge him? When you have nothing to lose, you are free to challenge a superior. And she asserts that if Jesus is truly compassionate, he can't turn away from her need. Dogs have rights.

In spite of her bravery, we should notice that the woman does not deny the category Jesus puts her in. She could have argued the point—and shamed Jesus. She did not say, *"Lord, I am not a dog, but a person."* She accepted the category but claimed that even at that level, she had rights.

(In their *The Mission and Message of Jesus* [E.P. Dutton, 1946], Major, Manson and Wright claim that the term used here for dog was not the usual term of contempt for the unclean dogs of the street, which was also used as a term applied to "unclean" persons such as Gentiles and Sodomites [Deut. 23:19; Rev. 22:15]. The term used is a double diminutive, not used elsewhere in the Gospels, and means "little dog"—one kept in the house. Thus, the term would not be quite as insulting as if the word for street cur had been used. It is an interesting but not ameliorating point.)

She used the debater's technique of latching onto what the person has said and turning it to her own advantage. A smart woman. A person so quick of mind she would have made a good lawyer. (How many Portias lost to sexism?)

Further, as I read the story, it seems that *this woman influenced Jesus.* Was he a limited Jew-healer, as he said, or one for all who needed healing? She prodded him to make a choice. Scripture says "Jesus grew in wisdom." How? Perhaps he grew in his self-understanding because of people like this woman. He matured in his concept of messiahship as she challenged him to recognize her need.

Traditionally we may have excused Jesus from the human necessity to make choices, to define himself, to mature in his own self-understanding, to interact with another person.

But there it is. Perhaps the message is that all downtrodden people, all uppity women, should take note. They should argue with conviction—even if it seems presumptuous. Sometimes humility is not in order. And being uppity is.

JESUS AND THE
ADULTEROUS MEN

John 8:1-11

Today some passages and stories in Scripture are being looked at with new awareness and new questions. How does a certain story, for instance, come across to a woman? Are there implications that traditional interpreters have not seen—or heard—or felt?

If you ask a group of women what passage about Jesus and women first comes to mind, one story is invariably mentioned. It is usually called, "The Woman Caught in Adultery." It could be called just as well, "Jesus and the Adulterous Men." Ostensibly it is about a woman, but basically it is about men and their double standard of morality.

A woman is brought before Jesus for his judgement. She has been "caught" or "taken" in the very act of adultery, we are told. The Pharisees remind Jesus that such a woman can be stoned according to the law (Dt. 22:23ff.). What does he think?

A woman reader or listener of this story may be granted an inward smile of amusement. A woman thinks: How could *the woman* be caught? It may not be apparent to everybody, but to a woman the act of adultery takes two.

How have church people for nineteen centuries accepted blindly a story that begins in this biased way—"a woman was caught"? By definition, adultery requires two persons who are not married to each other having sexual intercourse. To "catch" one person is like saying one person was caught playing tennis. One person can play golf, or solitaire. Or, in the sexual area, one person can masturbate. But two people share adultery.

Either the man committing adultery was a non-being, or he was so righteous that he was not regarded as being there in the act—though obviously he was there in the act. And there lies the probable explanation.

Perhaps in Jesus' day there existed a presupposition of guilt and condemnation associated with women and sexual sin, a predisposition so strong that people suspended the common facts of the situation in order to listen to a story like this. If the precondition of female guilt-association were not so ingrained in the culture's psyche, people would have laughed off the story as absurd. (A woman caught? Whom are you kidding?)

Such a bias did indeed exist in Jesus' day—a prejudgment against any woman who committed a sexual sin. And in those days, just as today, men were regarded less critically for sexual sins. For example Egyptian law states that a man who is "caught with a prostitute" is not imprisoned; instead, his testimony is used to convict and imprison the prostitute. (See *Sisterhood Is Global,* edited by Robin Morgan, Anchor Press/Doubleday, 1984, p. 197.)

Phyllis Trible tells four tales of woman abuse in her *Texts of Terror* (Fortress Press, 1984). Her portraits of suffering from ancient Israel are: Hagar, the slave used, abused, and rejected; Tamar, the princess raped and discarded; an unnamed woman, the concubine who was raped, murdered, and dismembered; and the daughter of Jephthah, a virgin slain and sacrificed (p. 1).

The question must be asked: *Where was the man* caught in adultery with the woman? Did he run away? Did he hide? So pervasive in Jewish society and in subsequent centuries was the acceptance of an anti-woman sexual bias that no one has asked this crucial question. (When I recently raised the question of the man's whereabouts to a large group of women, one woman suggested calmly, "He probably ran outside and picked up a stone.")

The Scarlet Letter, you remember, was also about a woman's guilt in adultery—a woman condemned, hated, ostracized by a community. She wore a letter "A" on her breast, for Adultery. In the story, Hester was blamed and her partner Dimmesdale went free. The community got its kicks out of (figuratively) kicking Hester. Hawthorne knew, however, that two persons were involved, and, further, that private guilt can destroy a person. In the novel, he skillfully showed, as a counterbalance to the serenity, self-forgiveness, and growth of Hester, the destruction of the co-sinner, Dimmesdale.

Jesus understood the problem of the adulterous men. He knew that guilt could not be assigned according to one's sex. He knew the men were guilty of sexual sins, and he proceeded to show the men their guilt.

To do this Jesus had to face not only a cluster of Pharisees who had brought the woman before him "to test him," but a crowd who had gathered to witness the confrontation. Maybe the woman was a political test case only. Maybe the testers wanted to put Jesus on the spot and did not intend to stone the woman. Maybe they would not have gone ahead with their prejudgment. Maybe. Whatever they intended, the woman before the crowd embodied a negative image, sin/sex...woman/Eve. Culture and religion had a scapegoat—a scapeshegoat—in the woman before Jesus.

See Jesus now as he takes hold of the drama. He is a leader, respected by the people. They wait. What will Jesus do? Will he lead the group in rock-throwing? Is he not a Jewish male, trained in the law as are other Jewish men? Is he not conditioned to see sex-guilt in woman and not to notice the participation of the male?

They watch Jesus as he leans down. Will he pick up a stone? He writes something in the sand. Something mysterious. The Scriptures do not reveal the secret writing. Did he write the adulterous man's name? Did he know the man? Had the woman been trapped by an angry husband? Did Jesus write the names of several men in the crowd who he knew had adulterous arrangements?

Whatever he wrote, it was *not* irrelevant. Christian interpretation has treated it as irrelevant. But we can assume it had something to do with the situation at hand, the situation of adultery.

And adultery was not uncommon.

Women in ancient Israel were regarded only in their relation to men, and were so readily associated with Eve/sex/sin that they were often assumed to be tempters. Men were conditioned to feel not guilty, to put the blame on women. Thus, to put down sin and temptation often meant to put down women. It was in this sort of atmosphere that Jesus took his stand.

The bystanders knew the law about adultery. Ironically, the commandment against adultery was directed at the Jewish male. He must not commit adultery with the neighbor's wife, the neighbor's *property*. The commandment was not concerned with the woman herself—what adultery did to her, whether she was a victim or cooperative partner, what her feelings of love or guilt or frustration might have been. The Jewish law specified that if a man had sex with a woman espoused to another man, he was bound to pay the other man (or a girl's father) for making a harlot out of her. That is, *he had damaged the other man's goods*. The rule was not concerned with her moral situation—only with how males perceived her. *She* was not recompensed as used, degraded, spoiled. She got no recompense for personal injury. The father or husband—the one whose propety she was—did. And if caught, she was to be stoned. (Only if a man had sex with a betrothed virgin was he also to be stoned. Apparently, if the woman was married, the adulterous man was not regarded as so blameworthy.)

The bystanders knew not only the laws, but the customs, the double standard for men and women. They knew the law admonished males against adultery, but chiefly punished females.

Although we don't know what it was that Jesus wrote in the sand, it was vital to the story action. He was somehow preparing the bystanders for his next move. Whatever he wrote dismayed the watching men. Then he spoke plainly.

"Let the one without sin cast the first stone."

The waiting accusers are shocked, disappointed, beaten, the men who are standing there waiting for a woman to be condemned. Through the centuries preachers have interpreted Jesus' challenge by saying he is charging us all with sin. But indeed, Jesus is specifically implying that the men before him are guilty of sexual sin.

Jesus is saying, "Men, it takes two. It takes two to commit this sexual sin. Your kind is guilty, too." Jesus has challenged their preconceptions. By his outrageous courage, by his effrontery, Jesus has charged fellow Jewish males with their own sexual misdeeds. Out of his confident self-knowledge he is saying that women are full persons due the same respect (and due process) as men. Jesus was challenging in one sentence the inbred assumptions and teachings of both culture and religion that the woman in sexual sin is more guilty than the male.

The men slink away. They had failed. Perhaps the Pharisees had not discussed how they would react if Jesus turned the encounter against them.

And then Jesus said to the woman, "Does no one accuse you?"

"No one."

She is free. Can you feel it, empathize with her freedom? Can you sense the gush of life coming into her mind and body? She had faced death from stoning. Had she felt resigned already to being beaten down with rocks and stones? Can one imagine a stone hitting one's face, one's breasts, the sharp edges cutting, making one's body run with blood? Do modern-day people stop to imagine such a horrible death, a death devised by ancient self-righteous persons as suitable for sexual sinners — especially a woman?

Jesus now tops this drama. The main point is yet to come. He has dealt with the men. Now he deals with the woman saved from a horrible death. He says two things. "Neither do I condemn you." And "Go and sin no more." Christianity has heard that one saying, but not the other.

For nineteen centuries Christendom has resounded with sermons on the admonition, "Go and sin no more." But rarely have sermons or ethical teachings been based on Jesus' first judgment, "Neither do I condemn you."

And it is a judgment. To be judgmental is usually given a negative connotation. But Jesus here gave a judgment that was not negative but positive. He says he does not condemn the woman for what the community was condemning her. *He gave a freeing judgment.* (The woman was not to wear an "A" on her breast.)

It is extremely important to notice that Jesus did *not* give the same freeing judgment to the men. His omission, indeed, is consistent with his saying elsewhere that harlots would go into the kingdom before Pharisees. He let the men go, but he did not say to them, "Neither do I condemn you."

He said it for the woman—the woman abused and degraded in a way the men were not. He gave her, and not the men, a positive and freeing judgment.

Christianity, it is apparent, has not known what to do with Jesus in his shocking judgment. On the one hand, he called the offense of both parties sin. "Go and sin no more." But he said authoritatively, "Neither do I condemn you."

No guilt for sexual sin? Surely Jesus can't mean that. Is not Christian history and doctrine full of condemnation of sexual sin? Doesn't sin require a negative judgment? Is there such a thing as condemnationless sin? Yes, Jesus had called it sin, but not condemned it. Is this our Jesus? Is this our religion?

Why has one saying been heard but not the other? I believe that the forgiveness, the non-condemning quality of his position is so unthinkable—so unrelated to most churchgoers' attitudes, that people have never accepted it. It is too much. One cannot sew it into the fabric of Judaeo-Christian morality. It is *too permissive.*

Jesus had let the men off— and no one has ever considered that this was too permissive a judgment. He let them walk away from probable murder. No one has suggested they should have been tried for attempted murder, for usurping the processes of justice. And even though Jesus did challenge the men with the self-knowledge of their own sins, no one—Bible scholar or theologian or preacher—seems to have noticed the men go scot-free, without a penalty.

Now Jesus lets the woman go with hardly a reproof. Jesus' saying that he does not condemn the woman has been too unacceptable for Christian people. It is too liberating. It does not fit their apparent need for a judgmental bias. And so Christianity has not bought it, has not taught it, has not internalized it—the astonishing idea that Jesus readily forgives sexual sin.

To accept that principle would allow people to be too free, too uninhibited. Would they not freely sin if they knew there would be no condemnation? If grace is free, then why not sin freely so that grace may abound? Even Paul could not resolve the question. He declared freedom from the law, but he established many rules for Christian behavior, apparently not trusting the hearts and wills of Christian persons to lead them aright.

If there is no condemnation, how can people be guided, managed? If women are not to be scapegoats for sexual sin/guilt, will men become responsible for their own conduct?

How can people be persuaded not to misbehave? Can men and women, all by themselves, decide to live a life with high principles—just out of joy and gratitude to God? Must both sexes have in their hearts the fear of punishment, of stoning and community rejection, in order to be motivated to be good? And can men give up the culturally reinforced feeling that in adultery the other sex is more guilty?

These questions are still before us as Christians. Christian men and women have not accepted the breakthrough challenge to responsibility: *Let him who is without sin cast the first stone.* Or the liberating sentence: *Neither do I condemn you.*

Women clutch at this story because, in the face of society's continuing double sex standard, they need the non-condemning affirmation of Jesus.

JESUS AND THE
WOMAN GOD-IMAGE

Luke 15:8-10

Today we are noticing that a cluster of cultural ideas can obscure an important meaning of a scriptural story.

Here is a story which Jesus tells about a woman looking for a coin she has lost. She sweeps until she finds it and then she calls her neighbors together to rejoice with her. Just so, says Jesus, there is joy before the angels of God over one sinner who repents.

What's so special here for women and men to understand today?

First of all, the position of the woman in the story. In this chapter Luke tells three Jesus stories that show how God is concerned for the lost. He will seek the lost, no matter how obscure the lost one is, no matter how much patience or persistence it takes.

We are all familiar with the stories—the lost son, the lost coin, and the lost sheep. In each story, someone represents God. As Leonard Swidler has pointed out in his previously cited article, "Jesus Was a Feminist," the woman, as well as the father and the shepherd, is in the God-position of looking for the lost.

"Oh, I never thought of that," most people are inclined to say. This aspect of the story has traditionally gone unnoticed. For centuries we have been deluged with sermons about the prodigal son and the lost sheep. But among the three stories, the poor woman sweeping for the coin gets swept under the carpet. Her story takes three verses; the prodigal son's takes thirty-three.

Why is the God-woman obscured?

First, because she is a woman. When we read or hear the story, our perception of it is immediately limited to the sex role implications we have all internalized. A person is a woman—*therefore* we look for significance in ways we are accustomed to thinking of women.

Women sweep. Women lose things. Women call together their neighbors for a celebration. These are familiar thought patterns. But we do not think: *the woman, like God, is seeking the lost.*

The seeking father of a son is a God/father symbol. The seeking shepherd is a God/caretaker symbol. And the woman is a God/housemanager symbol. But our first inclination in the coin story is to see just a woman doing something women do. Jean Baker Miller, in her *Toward a New Psychology of Women* (Beacon Press, 1976), notes that in a general way male society recognizes as activity only what men do. "Most so-called women's work is not recognized as real activity. One reason for this attitude may be that such work is usually associated with helping others' development, rather than with self-enhancement or self-employment. This is seen as *not doing anything.* Here again, we see how one's perceptions influence one's definition of what is happening and one's ability to call it by a name that (describes) what is happening" (p. 52).

Thus, in this story *a woman sweeping* is easier to accept than a *a woman God-figure seeking the lost.*

To see woman as God is to see the story in terms which shake up our familiar categories. To see a woman as God is to break out of our slots for women—our conditioned categories. Jesus did not have our hangups about picturing God as either sex. But because of our trained God-perceptions—the traditional association of God with the male sex—we have been unable to see in this story the woman as deity. We don't have room in our heads for that kind of woman.

Second, the God-woman is obscured because she is doing a housekeeping chore. Everyone knows that housekeeping chores are not important, either in a Jesus story or in a current social setting. Such tasks which are done in the seclusion of the home are not credited as being important to society. They are not part of the Gross National Product. (One of the complaints women are making today is that housework is not considered work, nor is it paid for or accorded any status. Cf. John K. Galbraith, "How the Economy Hangs on Her Apron Strings," *Ms.,* May 1974.)

What the God-woman was doing was regarded as non-essential labor, "women's work," both in the first century and in the twentieth century. The irony is obvious. If one cooks for one's family, it is not work. If one cooks for others, a paid job, it is work. If one does cleaning or child care for others it is considered work. If one does it for one's family, it is "not working." Traditionally whatever woman does is regarded as not worth pay or status.

Thus, what *this* woman does has been treated for centuries as unimportant. The emphasis has been that *she is merely sweeping for something,* not that *she is seeking the lost.* In the other two stories the main characters have jobs of importance. The father with the two sons is a man of some wealth, perhaps a large landowner and farmer. He has servants. The obedient son has been working faithfully for him. And the shepherd looking for the lost sheep is performing a respected labor in the community. But the woman is merely sweeping.

Thus, if the main character in a story is doing something generally regarded as trivial, it is easy to overlook that person's contribution and purpose. Her action, sweeping, is one which numbs the reader or listener from seeing behind the trivial job to the significance of what she is doing. One might call this mental block a cultural coverup.

Her purpose is to seek something that is lost. But the fact that she is a woman and her means of doing it—sweeping— have obscured the *why* of her action.

A related question can be raised: Would it be different if the woman were looking for a lost child? Would a seeking and forgiving mother be more highly regarded than a woman sweeping? Would she seem as significant as a father looking for a lost son? Or would people accustomed to the properness of sex roles shrug and say, "Oh, that is what mothers are for, to look for lost children and to forgive them. That's their nature." Carol Gilligan discusses this point in her book, *In a Different Voice* (Harvard University Press, 1982). She says that women not only define themselves in a context of human relationship but also judge themselves in terms of their ability to care. Woman has been a "nurturer, caretaker and helpmate, the weaver of those networks of relationships on which she in turn relies" (p. 17).

There is obviously no mother in the prodigal son story. The father takes the caring, forgiving position. And the father, it is implied, has reason to be *un*forgiving. After all, the son has squandered material wealth—wealth the father has earned or inherited. The son, by all means, should be cut off.

In contrast, the suggestion is often made in interpreting the coin story that the woman has obviously lost the cherished coin herself. Some sermonizing has focused on this idea—the woman's careless housekeeping. Yet is it not a bit curious that one never hears the parallel idea about the other two stories— that the father must have been a poor parent since his son left home, or that the shepherd must have been a careless shepherd since the sheep wandered off?

Beyond the obscuring of the story itself in Christian tradition, there is an element in the story which is overlooked.

The woman is looking for *money,* a very significant item. She is not looking for dust. She is not looking for a child. She is looking for money, a power item, the standard of value in the marketplace.

It is often suggested that the lost money was a wedding gift, part of a bride's necklace. This possibility has relevance to the position of women in Jesus' day. They had no rights of inheritance. Women were considered the father's or husband's property. If the coin was a bride's gift, it was perhaps part of her dowry, not necessarily the husband's or father's property. A dowry was necessary for a woman to be considered a desirable bride. The female person herself was not enough. One must have money to enhance one's value. Sometimes the woman had control of her dowry, or part of it, after marriage. And in some tribes or villages, if divorced, the woman got back some of her dowry.

Denied a source of money herself, the money she has is terribly important. Indeed the object of the search in each of the three stories is terribly important to the seeker: the son to the father, the sheep to the shepherd, the coin to the woman. Thus it is easy to see what Jesus was saying—that God cares terribly about the one who is lost.

Now then, if a woman can be the seeker in one of these stories of the lost, what does this do to our perception of God? Must we then question our usual tradition of identifying God in male terms? Apparently Jesus did not have our hangups about the sexuality of God. He pictured God as his spiritual parent, but he could use either sex as images of God.

There is another instance when Jesus used maternal imagery to describe his own relationship to his people: "O Jerusalem, Jerusalem, killing the prophets and stoning those who are sent to you! How often would I have gathered your children together as a hen gathers her brood under her wings, and you would not." Here we see motherly characteristics—caring, protectiveness, defensiveness, nurture, responsibility for others—all of which a parent of either sex can evidence.

Ancient deities were often goddesses. Throughout the history of civilization female deities have been worshiped. Even when the Judaeo-Christian concept of God developed, some of the so-called "female" type characteristics were still regarded as proper characteristics of God. Less and less emphasis has been placed on God as an avenging, eye-for-an-eye sort of God, and more and more emphasis on God as caring, loving and forgiving.

One insight gained from these three seeking stories is that the God qualities shown in them are human rather than strictly associated with either sex. Consider these characteristics displayed in the three stories:

Father Seeking	*Woman Seeking*	*Shepherd Seeking*
concern, anxiety	concern, anxiety	concern, anxiety
compassion	action, effort	action, effort
seeking, waiting	aggressiveness	aggressiveness
forgiving	achieving goal	achieving goal
rejoicing	rejoicing	rejoicing

There is no possibility that concern or anxiety can be identified with only one sex. Nor can "action" or "aggressiveness" in seeking a solution be identified with only one sex. Indeed, the father has the most passive role of the three. He stays at home and waits for the son to return. Only then does he rush out to greet him. He does not go out and seek. The other two protagonists take action to solve their problems. The woman sweeps. The shepherd searches.

This insight illustrates an awareness lesson which is becoming increasingly clear today—that sex roles are a limited way to look at persons. From these few stories one cannot conclude that waiting is for women only and action is for men only, or that God is limited to either waiting or action. If the woman and the shepherd are active, and the father is passively waiting, does this say something about God? Does it suggest that these qualities are interchangeable for the sexes, and that the sexes are interchangeable as images of God? Both women and men—as well as God—can show love and concern, or can aggressively perform an action to achieve a goal. God can passively wait for us, or he can initiate action to search for us and lead us. Luke in these three stories is showing us that God shares in many characteristics that we exhibit ourselves. As a spin-off, we are thus encouraged to be God-like.

We have been so used to thinking of certain characteristics as "appropriate" for one sex or another that it shatters our way of putting people in boxes to become aware that virtually all characteristics are human—and that women and men share in a common humanity. Strength, weakness, love, hate, concern, anger, violence, patience—all are human.

A book by two women seminarians, Emily Hewitt and Suzanne Hiatt, points out: "Once women become priests, it will be clear to all that many of the duties of a priest are duties which this society happens to consider as belonging in woman's realm. When a woman dons vestments we suddenly recognize that in this society they resemble more what women wear than they do the garb of men.... When a woman breaks bread and serves wine, then cleans the vessels when all have been fed, we suddenly recognize that she has served a meal and done the dishes, just as women do at home. When a woman hears confession or gives absolution we recognize that women are the listeners and comforters at home, too" (*Women Priests, Yes or No ?,* Seabury, 1973).

In these stories the formula is: A God-person is looking for the lost. It is simple. It is dynamic. Woman, man, shepherd—all have the searching, seeking, concern qualities that we expect of God.

The story of the God-woman can be explained as a parable which helps us see God's searching love—but also one which helps to liberate us from narrow concepts of men and women, as well as from a sexual pattern for God.

JESUS AND THE
AUDACIOUS WOMAN

Matthew 9:20-22; Mark 5:24-34; Luke 8:43-48

This is a loaded story—loaded with significance. Jesus' confrontation with the woman who had had a 12-year flow of blood is such a common story to Christians that it has become almost embarrassing. After all no one talks about women with a flow of blood. That's an intimate matter which should be kept between a woman and her physician.

People in Jesus' day were not so dainty. People knew about women when they had a flow of blood—either menstrual or continual. And it wasn't just curiosity. It was a situation that reflected the fear and prejudice and ignorance of first-century religion and culture. People knew when women menstruated because they were considered unclean by the religious community and were ostracized in cruel ways.

Indeed, attitudes about menstruation generally and menstrual blood specifically have been pervasive and negative. Most societies considered menstrual blood downright dangerous, especially to men, and established strict taboos to guard against its mystical properties. Psychologist Karen E. Paige points out in her article "Women Learn To Sing the Menstrual Blues" (*Psychology Today,* September 1973) that common taboos have prohibited menstruating women from cooking or preparing food for men, from participating in religious activities, and from having intercourse. Many societies, such as the Arapesh of New Guinea, even isolate women in specially built menstrual huts which are sometimes no larger than a few feet in diameter. The menstruating woman must maintain a crouched position during her isolation, and she is not allowed to eat, touch her body, sleep, or bathe. Above all, no man may come near her, for fear of his life.

Women who adhere to the Moslem, Hindu or Mosaic faiths must regard themselves as unclean in their time of menstruation and seclude themselves for a period. Medieval Catholicism made the stipulation that menstruating women were not to come into the church. Under the guidance of Dr. Marie B. Asaad, an Orthodox woman who is Deputy General Secretary of the World Council of Churches, the WCC engaged in a study, "Female Sexuality and Bodily Functions in Different Religions." The study asks pointed questions about menstruation, pregnancy, birthing, lactation, and menopause. It raises such issues as:

· How far do religious views, teachings and practices about women influence their role and participation in society?
· How comparable are the teachings among the religious groups? Are they central to the faith or not?
· Are the teachings open to fresh interpretations today in view of the changing status of women?

Says Asaad, "Personally I can't help but feel the contradiction between my church's teachings regarding female impurity and thus our exclusion from the Eucharist while menstruating—and Jesus' response to the woman who suffered from hemorrhage."

(For more information on the study, write Asaad at 150, Rt de Ferney, Ch 1211, Geneva 20, Switzerland.)

A forty-year-old woman I met in Japan in 1972, who was raised by her Russian Orthodox father, asked her father as a child why women could come only partway forward inside the church. He explained that they were menstruating and thus unclean. The woman said that she and her girlfriends were so ashamed when menstruating that they did not even want to go to church. As an adult she has continued to have acute feelings of unworthiness which she relates to this taboo.

Most people do not know that Orthodox Jewish women are still required to go to a special bath following their menstrual periods to be cleansed from their "uncleanness." Leonard Swidler and others note that this taboo is the basis for the Catholic Church not allowing a woman in the sanctuary during Mass—"she might be menstruating and hence unclean" (cf. "Jesus Was a Feminist," *art. cit.,* p 181).

The Old Testament laws concerning women's "uncleanness" are found in Leviticus 12 and 15, among other health and dietary laws. Women were not only unclean during their menstrual periods, but also for a week thereafter. A male, however, who had a nocturnal emission was considered unclean *only until evening.* Women were considered unclean also after childbirth. They were unclean for 7 days after giving birth to a boy, 14 days after giving birth to a girl. As if that were not enough disgrace, they were subjected to a "purification period" of 33 days for the the birth of a boy, 66 days for the birth of a girl, during which they were not allowed to enter the worship area. Thus the day she was born a daughter was bad news for her mother—causing 80 days of restrictions. The ultimate humiliation was the sin offering which was required both after menstruation and after childbirth. The "priest shall make for her before the Lord the expiation required by her unclean discharge" (Lev. 15:30).

It is difficult to imagine what this sort of unclean/sin stigma did to the women of Jesus' day. Women were condemned to a feeling of being soiled and unworthy most of their adult life. Menstruation, a normal process, was equated with filth and uncleanness. The culture on the one hand demanded that women give birth again and again. Yet to give birth required quarantine, purification and a sin offering. Since there were no birth control measures the woman was constantly having babies, enduring her period of isolation, having menstrual periods and being ostracized, getting pregnant, and facing the whole cycle again.

Not only was the woman unclean, but anything and any person she touched was unclean. Not only did she feel degraded herself, but she felt responsible not to contaminate others. It is horrible to contemplate the almost constant negative feelings a woman must have had about herself.

Even though the people of ancient times did not understand women's natural functions, anthropologists note that restrictions laid on women reflected a fear and hatred of women's blood, women's cycles, women's mysterious ability to reproduce, and an association of sin with women, sex and the body. Although there were Old Testament health and dietary laws to which men were also subjected, restrictions on males were not comparable to the burdens put on women.

(Karen Paige notes in her previously cited article a report on 71 societies which suggests a relationship between certain sex taboos and the severity of restrictions that women underwent during menstruation, suggesting that the blood of menstruation symbolizes the blood of castration, and thus that men fear women and avoid them during menstruation.)

Since he could not afford to soil himself, the "good" Jewish male was expected to say to such a woman as the one with the 12-year flow of blood, "Begone, thou filthy woman!" Identified by her ailment as a social outcast, the taboo against such a woman was common knowledge in the community. Thus, what Jesus did was much more shocking to the community then we can possibly imagine.

Since Matthew, Mark and Luke all report the story, it must have been regarded as highly significant that Jesus was casting off, putting down, this deeply ingrained blood taboo. Jesus was defying the Jewish law by healing this intrusive person, by *not* rejecting her when she touched him, by treating her like a person and not a reject. He "makes a great to-do about the event," says Swidler, and "by immediate implication he rejected the uncleanness of women who had a flow of blood, menstruous or continual" ("Jesus Was a Feminist," *art. cit.,* p. 181).

Not only was the woman a victim of religious prejudice and community ostracism, she was also, as the Mark account notes, the victim of medical abuse. She "had suffered much under many physicians and had spent all she had, and was no better but rather grew worse." We can only speculate what physicians of the first century might have prescribed or done to the woman to "cure" her ailment. Whatever, it was common knowledge that the woman had made the rounds, that no doctor had been able to help her, and that she was indeed worse rather than better.

This aspect of the story has current significance since many cases of women being subjected to questionable medical practices are coming to light. One reads of forced sterilization of poor, welfare or minority women, of too drastic breast surgery for cancer when a lesser type of surgery might have been adequate, of denial of tubal ligations or hysterectomies to women because the doctor doesn't think they have had "enough" children, of denial of abortion to women even in desperate circumstances. One woman's magazine recently headlined an article, "It's Your Body, Not Your Doctor's."

One woman resident noted that in her hospital the incidence of cesarean sections was one in five of those women who had not had a section before, and one in three of all women giving birth there.

In her book, *A Woman in Residence* (Michelle Harrison, M.D. Penguin Books, 1982), Dr. Harrison cited a *New York Times* article of January 4, 1977, that described the high rate (sixty percent) of cesareans in Brazil among women delivering in private clinics: "'A substantial number of physicians in Brazil believe that the surgical delivery is the best method of childbirth—it causes no harm to the figure, it is quick, and it is a lot more profitable,' said Dr. Paolo Belfort de Aguiar, the former president of the Brazilian Federation of Gynecology and Obstetrics Associations" (pp. 193-194).

This Jesus story shows a woman who was victimized by an ignorant and prejudiced society and religion. In spite of her physical situation and psychological abuse, in spite of what she had gone through, she still hoped someone could help her.

She was a person who had courage, wisdom and decisiveness. Having heard about Jesus as one who had healing power, she reasons that if she merely touches this man or his garment she may be made well. It sounds naive to twentieth-century ears—as does the unclean syndrome—but that is what she believed. She acted on her supposition, touched the man—and lo, she felt herself healed. She could feel the flow of blood stop.

Note what happens. According to Luke Jesus sensed that some power had gone forth from him. He turns around and asks who touched him. The disciples (Luke gives the line to Peter) point out the crowd pressing about, implying that it is foolish to ask who touched him.

The woman is nervous. She knows what startling event has occurred. She knows Jesus means to single her out. In *The Mission and Message of Jesus,* Major, Manson and Wright assert that Jesus scrutinized the crowd in order to "detect the culprit." She comes in fear and trembling and falls down before him.

Consider what her reaction indicates about her feelings. She comes in fear and trembling. *She comes in fear and trembling.* She was afraid because she had touched him. She had dared to touch a person whom she was not supposed to touch. Her conditioning was thorough. *You bad, soiled, unclean, despised woman,* her conditioning said. *You cannot touch any man—or else you will cause him to be unclean. You have contaminated this Jesus. He will have to observe certain washing rituals because of you. And here you not only*

*have touched him, you have taken some of his healing power.
How dare you be so presumptuous? How audacious of you.*

Thus she thought within herself. She had internalized the condemnation of her society and religion. She was trained to despise herself because of her infirmity. She knew that in the judgment of her contemporaries *she was disgusting.* How could such a disgusting person make demands on a celebrity?

So, rather than whooping and hollering with joy that she was healed, she groveled before Jesus. Rather than calling out to him in joyous thanks that he had healed her, she kneels and apologizes for having the nerve to touch him.

Forgive me for wanting to be healed. Forgive me for wanting to be clean—and to be regarded as clean by my peers. Forgive me for having the nerve to act in my own behalf, for touching you, for seeking your help. Forgive me for bothering you. Forgive me for using your power without asking you. I was sneaky. I was afraid you would reject me as you have a right to do, afraid that my touch would make you unclean.

But rather than condemn her, Jesus tells the woman her faith has made her whole. He knows that singling her out has embarrassed her. But even so, he is willing to take a public stand against an evil taboo, and he knows the crowd will take notice.

The woman is reborn, given a new life. No longer will she be regarded as filthy, as unclean, as disgusting. Can we imagine it? No longer will she be bothered with the mechanics of taking care of her daily, nightly problem. No longer will she have to seek out doctors for a cure. No longer will she be rejected by the community.

We can acknowledge that this is a beautiful story—a bit embarrassing, but touching because Jesus dared community standards to affirm a poor outcast woman as a human being. How nice. We are smugly thankful that modern society is enlightened as far as women's menstrual cycles are concerned.

The United States does not relegate menstruating women to special huts, but, as Karen Paige observes in her previously cited article, we have our share of superstitions, and the implicit belief lingers that the menstruating woman is unclean. Many couples abstain from sex during the woman's period, and women take great care to avoid any signs of menstruation which would cause profound embarrassment to the woman and the observer. Sanitary napkin and tampon ads perpetuate—and try to placate—such apprehensions. These commercials assure the girl or woman that she will be safe from public humiliation. All women are under pressure to maintain high standards of "feminine hygiene" during the menstrual flow. In *The Female Eunuch* (Bantam Books, 1971), Germaine Greer notes that the chief success of tampons is that they are not only convenient but hidden. She remembers carrying pads and pins for six months before her period started in order to be prepared. Greer also notes the contradiction in attitude that regards menstruation as divinely ordained and yet unmentionable.

Today there is a multimillion marketing effort to encourage women to wear pads every day of the month. "Their marketers have decided to teach women that they are unclean," says Emma Hill, an analyst with Wertheim & Co. "The market could be enormous if they are successful."

Sales of sanitary pads have taken off since 1980 when toxic-shock syndrome was linked to tampon use. The market is valued at $730 million a year now, and pad makers are battling to increase their share with expensive ads.

Manufacturers are counting on women's concern with cleanliness to increase pad sales; ads stress products' absorbency and urge women to use pads more frequently to absorb dampness, etc.

Johnson & Johnson offers twelve types of pads and has come out recently with three more. Tampax has just put four new products on the market. Total ad spending for pads jumped to $68.5 million in 1982, up from $38.1 million two years earlier (*Wall Street Journal,* Dec. 3, 1983).

Fear of sexuality, of which menstrual taboos are a part, is a common element of our social conditioning. Both boys and girls are conditioned to be slightly ashamed of their sex organs and of sex. Classical philosophers like Augustine counseled that intercourse was only justified for procreation. And Pope Paul in *Humanae Vitae* said about the same thing—that each sex act must be open to the possibility of pregnancy. (That is, if you insist on indulging in sex, you must be willing to pay the price of having a baby.) And of course Mary, the ultimate woman image, is projected as "pure" precisely because she became pregnant without normal sexual intercourse. She jumped from virgin to mother in one "clean" leap. (One wonders if the Church Fathers ever debated the theological necessity of also relieving Mary of the uncleanness of menstruation.)

A woman obviously gets the brunt of this fear of sexuality. Just as in classical times woman was identified with the "lower half" of the human being's experience (body, sex, sin) and the male was identified with the "upper half" of human nature (spirituality, intellectuality), today the mystique lingers on in the sexist structures of society. A woman is excluded from virtually all top level jobs in government, business, religion, education, etc., while conditioned to be content with what she symbolizes to the male perception—a glamorous homebody surrounded by children, doing the servant work of the home, the church, the community, the professions and the business world. Either as sex object or on a pedestal she is out of the way and not to be taken seriously.

Thus, says Rosemary Radford Ruether, in "Sexism and the Theology of Liberation" (*Christian Century,* Dec. 12, 1973), the cult of true womanhood, which idealizes the role of woman as a glorified servant, is an essential part of the ideology of modern industrial society. If a woman breaks out of these socially approved images, she is regarded as something of a freak, as unfeminine, as aggressive and competitive.

What I am saying is that although we have no overt blood taboo, we have its equivalent. Women are barred, rejected, and considered inappropriate for certain places and pursuits. Today women ministers are becoming more acceptable in several mainline Protestant churches, and the percentage of women in seminaries has increased dramatically since 1970. Among Catholics, the Women's Ordination Conference and other coalitions have developed large followings with a chief goal to achieve the ordination of women to the priesthood. However, women are still excluded from having an effective voice and power in the ruling cliques of every institution of society.

This exclusion is partially based on women's traditional association with sexuality, sin, reproduction and its attendant cultural myths—that woman is weak, non-intellectual, inferior, needs protection, etc.

Although women today are not able to "touch Jesus" physically, they can be audacious in other ways. Just as they are insisting on equality in churches and employment and are seeking political office and justice in the law, they are becoming educated in theology, invading the chancels of the churches, and walking out when subjected to the reading of repressive passages or demeaning sermons. No longer pressured to have large families, they can be more audacious in asserting their other talents wherever they see the opportunity. (Indeed, a new medical technique called "menstrual extraction" may foreshadow a future in which women may have an "extraction" on the first day of their monthly periods, thus avoiding the bother and burden of the monthly "curse." One wonders why medical science—so eager to pursue test-tube fertilization and cloning—has not tried to alleviate or eliminate menstruation. Or has childbirth as punishment so entered our thinking that we dare not tamper with part of the reproductive cycle—menstruation?)

Like the woman who dared to latch on to Jesus, today's woman must step out of the unclean role. To reject uncleanness is to move into the mainstream of church and society. There must be no more holding back out of a false sense of shame and guilt. Christian women must declare that they do not feel guilty for "touching Jesus," for using his power. Women must accept the responsibility of being singled out as real people. True change in church and society will come when women no longer feel embarrassed, when they can act as audacious, normal persons. Only then can whole persons— women and men together—share leadership and servant responsibilities, based on ability and not on limiting sexual stereotypes.

JESUS AND THE
UTERUS IMAGE

Luke 11:27

Here is a story, more or less ignored for centuries, which has importance today in relation to the women's movement. The women's movement is saying: Let's look beyond the *body-function* of women to the *person*.

In Jesus' day as well as ours a woman was honored because of her reproductive capacity—she would have babies and nourish them. In this story, a woman comes up and cries out, "Blessed is the womb that bore thee and the paps which thou has sucked." That's the King James Version. New English has it: "Happy the womb that carried you and the breasts that suckled you!"

In modern terms the woman might have said: "You're a great man, Jesus, but let's give credit to the uterus and breasts that got you started. Let's bless Mary's reproductive system without which you wouldn't be here."

Jesus puts down this concept. *"Yea, rather is the person blessed who hears God's will and does it."* Jesus is not content with the usual stereotyping of a woman in Jewish society of the first century. Rather than uterus/breasts, he sees the whole person—a woman who has a mind, spirit and will.

To get a balanced perspective of such body-praise, imagine someone coming up to a man who has an outstanding son and saying, "Blessed is the semen which fertilized your wife's egg." Or, "Blessed is the male organ that participated in the act which led to conception." Is this any more ridiculous than praising Mary's breasts and uterus?

Subsequent centuries have been so accepting of the stereotyped woman that they have not noticed what Jesus said. Religious interpreters have not known what to do with this radical rejection by Jesus of the uterus image. Does he mean to put down the idea of woman as child-bearer? Is he demeaning her function as a fetus-carrier and a baby-suckler?

Remember that only if a woman had children, and preferably boys, was she honored. If she were "barren" she was regarded as one to be pitied. Actually her status in that society was based on the uterus image. Her worth *was* in her procreativeness.

In a recent attitude survey done by the Lutheran Church in America (Office of Bishop, 231 Madison Ave. New York, May 1985), one statement said: "Raising children is the most important thing a woman can do." In response, 54% of respondents agreed, while 31% disagreed and 15% were undecided. And while 38% of respondents believe a mother should have primary childcare responsibility, 48% felt a woman has just as much right as a man to have a job outside the home.

It is mind-blowing to realize that Jesus was actually rejecting the commonly accepted justification for the existence of woman. If not a child-bearer, what was woman? Jesus is saying: *She is one who can hear the will of God and do it.*

Until recent years people have not noticed very much that woman has been treated as if her pregnancy/birth/child-care abilities were her justification for being. Men, obviously, are not justified by their participation in procreation. Their participation is regarded as almost incidental. Men have individual purposes in life apart from fatherhood. But most women have been regarded as birth vessels primarily.

Harriet Taylor Mill said over a hundred years ago: "To say that women must be excluded from active life because maternity disqualifies them for it is in fact to say that every other career should be forbidden them in order that maternity may be their only resource" (*Essays on Sex Equality,* University of Chicago Press, 1970, p. 104).

The major writers of Christendom accepted the stereotyped woman. Said Martin Luther, "What if women should die in childbirth? That is what they are here for, to have children."

Mary has been especially looked at in this limited way. Mary obviously is not the model of normal, sexually-relating womanhood. Rather, she has been a model for motherhood. She was projected to Christians as skipping from virginity to motherhood with no sex in between. What do women hear? That to be virtuous is to be a virgin—and a mother. Sex is not even in the picture.

The Catholic tradition has even taught that Mary and Joseph lived as brother and sister and had no other children. Scripture references to Jesus' brothers and sisters really meant "cousins." Although Protestant churches have taught that Mary and Joseph did have children, they have not stressed the normal married relationship between Mary and Joseph. (It is interesting to note that Jesus never refers in Scripture to his parents as other than normal parents, nor does he ever refer to a virgin birth.)

To first-century people, to look upon a woman as childbearer was so common that it was not at all surprising for the woman to come up to Jesus and praise his mother's breasts and uterus. She may have expected him to be pleased. What was surprising was that Jesus differed with her.

Note that the woman doesn't say, "Blessed be the sex act which brought you into the world." It was the sex act itself which had to be omitted, put down, in order to make Mary a "holy" person. To the first-century mind, with its cultural emphasis on spirituality vs. carnality, woman and sex were often associated with sin. Manichaeism emphasized the dual nature of human beings—a higher nature which devoted itself to the spiritual life, and the lower nature which included one's sexual desires.

Thus, for Mary to be "pure" she must be regarded as a virgin whose pregnancy was of God, not caused by intercourse with a man. Today we can understand the emphasis on her virginity, breasts and uterus as due to the cultural conditioning of the times.

It is this labeling that Jesus rejects. He is saying for all who can hear—and notice—that a woman as well as a man can hear the Word of God and do it. An absolutely stunning declaration.

Jesus did not want women to be put in a slot because of their biology. He saw all persons as individuals who are to hear the Word and do it. Yet our sexist blinders have prevented our seeing this affirmation of personhood for women.

The message is exciting for women today who have felt that their only worth was in bearing children. With the emphasis on overpopulation and the consequent downswing in population, and with more emphasis on use of birth control and planning one's family, women realize that they have other functions in life—they are free to choose other options. Jesus is saying: You have a meaning, a focus to your life other than the traditional one of child-bearing.

I don't think Jesus means to demean family or the part that both men and women have in reproduction. He spoke too kindly of children and of home life for that to be implied. Rather, he is emphasizing that (1) having children is not all of life, and that (2) hearing and doing God's will is the chief goal for both sexes.

Today's woman, with a 78-year life expectancy, is learning that in her long life she has room for both family concerns as well as other options.

JESUS AND THE
MINISTERING WOMAN

Matthew 26:6-13; Mark 14:3-9;
Luke 7:36-50; John 12:1-8

Woman as sinner. That is the label for the person who anoints Jesus at Simon's house, kisses his feet and wipes them with her hair. Simon the leper is appalled that Jesus calmly accepts attention from such a person. If he were really a prophet, Simon thinks, he should know what sort of person this woman is. Jesus, rebuking Simon with a story about a lender who had two debtors, chides him for not administering to Jesus himself, and then proceeds to commend the ministering woman and forgives her sins.

An innovative way to view the drama is to consider it in the light of "I'm OK, You're OK." Although transactional analysis is a modern way of looking at social interchanges, it is helpful to see the Luke story as a game which the people at Simon's dinner were playing.

First of all the woman by her ministering actions was saying, "Jesus, you are OK." Simon by his judgmental thoughts was saying that the woman was not OK. And he wondered inwardly if Jesus was OK, since Jesus obviously did not see the woman as a sinner. Jesus said to Simon, "You are not OK, but this woman is OK because she is ministering to me." Then Jesus tells the woman she is OK. Simon however still feels OK—even when told plainly by Jesus he is not OK. And finally, the men guests question whether Jesus is OK since he claims a power of forgiveness they are not ready to grant him.

All four Gospels have some version of this story. In Matthew, Mark and John the complaint against the woman centers on the cost of the ointment and the question: Why wasn't the ointment sold and the money given to the poor? In the Luke version which concerns us here, the interest focuses on three elements: (1) the woman's actions, (2) Jesus' response to her actions and to Simon's negative attitude, and (3) the guests' reaction to Jesus pronouncing forgiveness for the woman.

In all four accounts *what the woman did* is not really accepted except by Jesus. In all four accounts what she did is obscured either by a discussion of what could have been done with the money she spent, or by concern about her sinner status. Whatever she did was as if it were not happening.

Simon the host was so conscious of woman as sinner that he did not see what she did except to be offended by it—and to wonder why Jesus was not offended. This woman had broken the rules and under the system of patriarchy rules and laws were more important than relationships and compassion.

As Carol Gilligan points out (previous citation, pp. 30-32), boys and men are socialized to make moral decisions based on rules and laws, while girls and women base their reasoning on relationships, establishing connections and communication with others.

This woman felt love, compassion, a warm response to Jesus and his ministry. Because of her response to him, she takes action. She is assertive and daring to enter such a judgmental, hostile environment. To Simon and the by-sitters, her ministering act could obviously be of no value because of her bad name in the community. Simon put her down in his mind ("not OK"), seeing her through a dirty filter of sin/sex/woman/Eve. Simon and his friends did not see her *act* because of her label. They had pictures in the head which made her a non-person. She didn't count.

The woman has no name. It is interesting to note the different translations of the woman's label. RSV calls her "a

woman of the city who was a sinner." The New English Bible
says that she was "a woman who was living an immoral life."
The Living Bible calls her "a woman of the streets—a prostitute." And Philips terms her "a woman known in the town as a
bad woman." All are *not OK* terms.

Jesus however did not see a stereotype before him, but a
woman who was ministering to him. She was doing something
for Jesus—touching him, kissing him, putting ointment on
him, wiping his feet with her hair. And he was not embarrassed.
Jesus perceived these acts as acts of devotion and ministry and
love.

There are three implications of the story that Christianity
has missed. Traditionally, Christian interpretation has blanked
out or veiled *what the woman did* and concentrated on a
discussion of her sinner status, or on what should have been
done with the money, or on what the anointing meant for
Jesus' coming burial. Christian preaching has tended to see the
woman as Simon saw her—a sinner—or as the disciples saw
her (in John it is Judas)—as wasting money on a foolish
gesture. Jesus however saw a ministering woman whose kisses,
tears and anointing he accepted with satisfaction, if not pleas-
ure. And he saw Simon as an insensitive host who did not
recognize his own deeds of omission. Note that Jesus was
quick to preach at Simon—but not at the woman. And even
when he forgives her sins, he did not preach at her or condemn
her. He merely forgives her.

Second, traditional Christianity has not noticed that in this
story Jesus was passive in receiving what the ministering
woman did. He did not act. She initiates action and he responds
to her action. Nor did Simon act, but he inwardly thought
put-down thoughts to which Jesus responded verbally. Christianity has not noticed that in truth the whole story is based on
the actions of an assertive demonstrative woman.

Perhaps Christian interpreters have not looked at the
story in this way because they—and we—do not expect Jesus

to receive from others. We expect him to give, to preach, to teach, to suffer. We do not expect him to receive or be benefited by others. This is a religious stereotype which parallels a social sex stereotype. That is, we are socially conditioned not to expect men to be passive or women to be active in a self-assertive sense. People who stray from such a sex norm are usually explained in some way. When women act decisively they are "busybodies" or "pushy" or "bitches." When men are passive, they are "strong and silent" or "tempted" or "great intellects or artists." In this way stereotypes control us by controlling our expectations. Jesus as passive receiver and woman as minister do not fit our expectation patterns.

The third implication missed by Christian interpretation is that sexual purity is not a prerequisite for ministering to Jesus. The woman symbolizes freedom from the "sinner" stereotype.

Picture the scene—a private dinner with many guests. A private dinner in Palestine was not so private that uninvited guests were excluded. Perhaps many people came in and out, interacting with guests who reclined on couches. Guests would have removed their sandals as they came in, their bare feet stretched away from the table. One can imagine the woman entering almost unnoticed, pouring her ointment on Jesus' feet, weeping, wiping his feet and kissing them. She had a plan of action and she followed it through. As this went on, one can imagine that she drew more and more attention.

Perhaps the woman had already known Jesus, having met him as he went about the countryside. Perhaps he had done something which touched her. There is no indication in Luke's account as to whether she was a stranger or whether some acquaintance precedes this encounter. (The story in John which places the incident in the home of Mary and Martha and Lazarus and assigns the action to Mary assumes an established Jesus-Mary relationship, but it does not refer to Mary as "sinner.")

Simon is put off by the woman's attentions to Jesus. Can't Jesus see she is not OK? If Jesus were really a prophet he would know what sort of person the woman is. Jesus responds to Simon's thoughts (Luke intends us to accept Jesus' ability to read another's thoughts) with a story about a lender and two debtors. Since one debtor owed much and one owed only a small amount, when the lender "forgave" the debts, which would love him more? Simon answered correctly—the one who owed most. Jesus tells the story to make a point in relation to the woman, but first he rebukes Simon who had not brought water for Jesus' feet, who had not kissed his feet, who had not anointed him with ointment. All these things the woman had done, and now Jesus compares her to the person whose large debt was wiped out. She who has loved much, and who has many sins, now has her sins forgiven.

(Note that there are two side issues here which are somewhat provocative. (1) The "point" of the parable is inconsistent with the story. Does love precede forgiveness, as for the woman, or—as in the parable—does forgiveness lead to love in response? And (2) if as some suggest, Simon was one of the lepers Jesus had healed, then his debt to Jesus was immense. Jesus could have been implying that he should have loved much in response, and thus the woman's act was more striking in comparison.)

The male guests are stunned. "Who does he think he is," as The Living Bible puts it, "going around forgiving sins?" Surely, Jesus was meeting the woman's extravagant action with an extravagant concession. It seemed arrogant.

There is quite a contrast to notice. Jesus reproaches Simon for being insensitive, for not washing his feet, for not kissing him, for not being concerned about his well-being. In contrast to Simon's non-actions, Jesus makes a great to-do about the woman's actions. She is OK.

Notice the verbs: She wet his feet with her tears. She

wiped them with her hair. She kissed his feet. She anointed his feet with ointment. (In both Matthew and Mark she pours it upon his head.) Although she is providing the ministering, Jesus responds verbally to her demonstration, her ministry to him. He praises her extravagantly. He commends her as an example to these self-righteous males—one, at least, a Pharisee who should be an example of righteousness.

Although Jesus forgives the woman's sin it is interesting to note that she has not asked for forgiveness. Some interpreters have assumed her penitence and that her devotion was an act of penitence. (One commentator even labeled the passage "Jesus and a Penitent Sinner.") Simon of course was seeing what he had been programmed to see—a sinner woman who was an offense to his morals, who was disrupting his entertainment of dinner guests. He saw a woman with a label. She belonged in a slot, a category.

Simon also *heard* what he was programmed to hear. He does not hear Jesus' reproaches. Simon is so unaware of what Jesus is saying to him that he is not even apologetic for not doing what he should have done as a good host. Had he provided footwashing for other guests and not for Jesus? Was he merely a careless host? Was it the duty of some slave who goofed off? We do not know. Apparently neither Simon nor the other guests felt any guilt for not honoring Jesus as someone special. They feel OK. But they do show astonishment at Jesus' claims to forgive sins. They are astonished that Jesus treats this sinner woman as a person, that he accepts her actions as if they are important, as if they mean something. That is not OK/acceptable to them.

Anthropologists note that although what women do and what men do varies from society to society, generally whatever women do is regarded as less important than what men do. Certainly, in this case, whatever a sinner woman does (besides her sin) is not regarded as very important. Once a woman is known as a sinner, her other activities pale into insignificance. It does not seem important to these men that a lowly woman is performing an act of devotion to Jesus.

Yet the woman is the active, initiating force of the whole drama—a drama so well known that some version of it is reported in all four Gospels.

Why did the woman's ministering action make the men feel uncomfortable—so uncomfortable that attention was called either to her reputation or to the extravagance of her gift? Compare her action, for instance, with the action of the wise men. Because the wise men brought gold, frankincense and myrrh to the newborn Jesus, it has never been suggested that these gifts were wasteful and might better have been spent to serve the poor. What is the difference? The gifts in both instances were lavish measures of awe and devotion. They were both for the same person—Jesus. The ointment poured on Jesus' feet and the gold, frankincense and myrrh brought to the Bethlehem babe were extravagant. The woman's gift was given for what Jesus *was*—prophet, leader, healer. The other gifts were brought in honor of who he was *to become*. Is the difference one of *who gave the gifts*, of sexual stereotypes? Important wise males were OK status persons in the area of Palestine. The sinner woman, in contrast, was a not OK low status person, foolish, unwise, one about whom questions could be raised. Her act could be discounted.

In first-century patriarchal social structure, women were regarded as little more than slaves, and the woman who transgressed the boundaries of acceptability was treated with harshness both by social custom and by religion. Unlike the woman, self-important males like Simon were inclined to feel little guilt either for complicity in adultery or for prostitution, as well as no guilt for failing to perform a social courtesy like ministering to a hot and dusty guest.

Jesus quite plainly is telling Simon that this woman Simon has labeled bad *is superior to him*. This is so unacceptable an idea that Simon does not grasp it, does not internalize what Jesus is saying. Simon-males see no need to change, to accept criticism—or to see a "bad woman" in a new light. They are so accustomed to feeling not guilty, so used to laying blame on women of the street that Jesus' reproach does not even register, does not meet any chord of response in them.

Perhaps we are expecting too much for Simon to have seen with Jesus' eyes that the woman was ministering, that Simon and his friends were judgmental and inattentive—and why Jesus was so impressed by the woman. It is not too much, however, to expect modern Christians to identify with the perception of Jesus rather than that of Simon.

Putting the story in "OK, not OK" terms shows how easily Jesus' contemporaries attached a "sin" label to a woman, and how this prejudiced their reactions. Many concerned Christians today—feminist scholars, writers and theologians—are noticing that negative images from Scripture are still being used to denigrate women while many positive passages are ignored, passed over lightly or interpreted to support still-existing stereotypes.

For example, commentators generally ignore the crucial role that women played at the birth of Moses. They simply take the women in the story for granted. They consider it natural for women to be concerned with birth and children. (Letty Russell, *The Liberating Word,* Westminster, 1976, pp. 64-65).

The actions of the women, indeed, have a theological significance. Says Russell:

"The disobedience of the midwives saves the Hebrew people; the disobedience of the mother, sister, and Pharaoh's daughter saves Moses. If God was later acting through Moses to deliver the people, then God first of all acted through these women to deliver the people. Women as well as men are God's agents of salvation and, in the story of the exodus, God's first agents." See also the long poem, "Wit and Wisdom of the Midwives," in *Eve and After* by Thomas John Carlisle (Wm. B.

Eerdmans, 1984, p. 33), in which he calls them "the powerless who used the power they had—we hail them as the staunch inaugurators and initiators—the founding fore- and foster-mothers of exodus and liberation...."

For another example, Diana Lee Beach in "Fun with Dick and Jane," a study of church school materials sponsored by six Protestant denominations, says: "The women who most often appear in Bible stories are Eve, Gomer, Jezebel, the woman taken in adultery, Mary Magdalene—all women explicitly connected by these authors with sexual wickedness. Even the few good women who appear are portrayed as passive, obedient, humble, waiting, acted upon—virtues which women certainly do not need to have reinforced. Where are Deborah, Rahab, Mary and Martha—all women of intelligence, resourcefulness and courage? The image of moral weakness, passivity and inferiority prevails even though the Gospels clearly record that Jesus vigorously upheld the dignity and equality of women in the midst of a very male-dominated society, addressing their spiritual natures, entrusting them with his teachings and going against custom and the law to do so" (*Spectrum/International Journal of Religious Education,* Sept.-Oct. 1971).

(Since medieval times Mary Magdalene has been one of the most maligned women in the New Testament, largely because some scholars of an earlier period chose to identify her with the unnamed sinful woman of Luke 7:36-50 who ministered to Jesus. There is no evidence that Mary Magdalene was a harlot. At most she was neurotic. John gives her the leading part in the resurrection narrative. She is sent forth with the message: "Go and tell." See Edith Deen, *All the Women of the Bible* [Harper & Bros., New York, 1955], pp. 200ff. Also, James Hastings, *Dictionary of the Bible* [Charles Scribner's Sons, New York, 1963], pp. 628-629.)

How can we emphasize the positive? We can identify with the women whom Jesus affirmed and insist on their strong qualities. In this story a woman ministers to Jesus, performing an act of love and recognition which he interprets as anointing for his burial. Rather than a spontaneous display as some would have it, her act was premeditated quite carefully—for who would carry around such expensive ointment? She supported her feelings with deliberate planning. For the woman at Simon's house, *thought* plus *emotion* equals *act*.

In this story of the ministering woman, then, Christendom has missed several things: the initiative of the woman, the passive as well as the verbal responses of Jesus to her initiative, and the implication that neither sex identity nor sexual purity is a prerequisite to performing a service for Jesus.

Rather than emphasize the woman's sinner label or what could have been done with her money, the interpretive emphasis should be on the activity of the woman based on her own purposeful decision to enter Simon's house with a plan in mind. Jesus' response to the woman not only leads to a verbal rebuke of Simon as judgmental and unforgiving, but indicates love, acceptance and forgiveness for the woman.

We do not know if Jesus' forgiveness of the woman in Simon's house wiped out her label in the community. Probably not.

(Simon, it is interesting to note, provides an example of labeling or stereotyping of a peculiar type. Known as Simon the leper in the Mark account, it is assumed that he had been cured of leprosy, perhaps by Jesus. But Simon is not treated as a leper anymore, although the label hangs on. His health now established, he was no longer contagious or untouchable. Thus in his situation, naming or labeling as a way to set a person apart had lost its clout. "Simon the leper" was an empty but familiar title. One wonders whether a label based on a physical illness was as damaging and persistent as one based on sexual sin.)

Jesus' final comment about this important unnamed woman is that what the woman has done will be "told in memory of her." It is ironic that what the "woman has done" has been so forgotten that we do not even know her name.

Elisabeth Schussler Fiorenza observes in her book named for this woman (*In Memory of Her,* Crossroad, 1983, p. xiii) that of the three disciples figuring prominently in the passion account, everyone knows of Judas who betrayed Jesus and Peter who denied him, but the woman is virtually forgotten. This memorable woman and her "prophetic sign-action did not become a part of the gospel knowledge of Christians." Perhaps with our current ability to cast off traditional bias regarding women, we can appreciate the remarkable women in Jesus' life and thus lift to a higher level of respect this particular woman who ministered to Jesus.

If we can separate her sinner label from her act of ministry, we see a model for women—women today who are certainly no strangers to being the foot-wipers, the person-ministers, anointers of Christendom.

JESUS AND THE
WIFE IMAGE

Matthew 22:23-33; Luke 20:27-38; Mark 12:18-27

Women have been thought of chiefly as relatives of men. Women are daughters of men, wives of men, mothers of men, sisters of men. In first-century society the wife image was the most important and the most accepted way of defining a woman. A man had a wife—and a house and servants and oxen and asses. In the Ten Commandments the male is instructed not to covet his neighbor's house or his wife or his ox or his ass, etc. The wife ranks second, along with the servants and cattle. She was part of his property, his baggage, his possessions.

The Sadducees, in an incident reported by Matthew, Mark and Luke, come to Jesus with a question about a woman who is a wife. A certain woman had been married successively to seven brothers and has borne no children. In heaven whose wife would she be? According to the levirate marriage law (Dt. 25:5-10), when a husband died, it was the duty of his brother to marry the widow "and perform the duty of a husband's brother unto her." If the dead brother and the woman had had no children, then the first child of the subsequent marriage would be considered the child of the first husband.

The purpose of levirate marriage was to perpetuate the male lineage. There seems to have been no concern for the feelings involved, whether the woman cared for the brother or despised the brother, or whether the brother might have disliked the wife of his dead brother. Lineage, not personal affection, was the overriding principle. As Deuteronomy says, "his widow shall not marry outside the family." A wife was the means of propagation who could be passed from brother to brother. She belonged to the family. Thus it was possible that a woman could have a childless marriage with each of seven brothers. The Sadducees, by describing such a situation, thought they had a logical question to confound Jesus. Since marriage meant "belonging" as a possession and the woman had "belonged" to seven brothers, whose wife would she be in the resurrection?

Now the Sadducees did not believe in the resurrection. They felt this hypothetical question was a way to prove that a future life was ridiculous. Since the Pentateuch did not give any basis for the belief in a future life, and the Sadducees (like the Samaritans) believed only in the Pentateuch, they felt that if Moses had intended a belief in the resurrection he would have plainly said so.

It was a trick question. Like the Jews, the Sadducees thought of a wife as one who belonged to the husband with whom she had children. Even without children, in his life she would have been the property of the man to whom she was married. After this life, the Sadducees believed, the whole system of passing a wife from brother to brother would break down.

With such a legalistic example, the questioners hoped to make a fool of Jesus. Jesus, they thought, could not deny the force of the levirate obligation. He must admit that the brothers were following their obligation to the woman and to the family. Thus, the question would stump him. How could a woman have seven husbands in a future life? (When a culture sees a woman/wife in a servant, subordinate position, its mental concepts are limited.)

Jesus surprised the Sadducees by saying they do not know their Scripture and that they do not understand what the resurrection is all about. In heaven men and women are not given in marriage. They are all equal to the angels, separate beings, separate identities. They are spiritual beings.

Recalling Moses' reference to God as the "God of Abraham, Isaac and Jacob" (Ex. 3:6), Jesus says that these ancestors who have been dead several hundred years, must be living in a future life already. According to Major, Manson and Wright (*op. cit.*), they were "alive in God's presence."

Jesus was giving a two-part answer, an answer which disturbed the Sadducees. Not only did the Sadducees not want to view Abraham, Isaac and Jacob as alive in a spiritual sense, they did not want to view a woman as other than a man's possession—either in this life or in a later life. To them Abraham, Isaac and Jacob were dead: their bodies were in the ground. To them, a woman in heaven could not have equal status to a man. These hair-splitting men could only view a dead person as dead and a woman as a possession. How could one imagine dead ancestors as living still? And how could one imagine a future life without first-century marriage relationships? Their imaginative powers were limited. They could not absorb the idea that Jesus was saying that in heaven the woman and the man would be regarded in a different way from the usual earthly ranking.

What does a woman hear in this story?

To make the story more graphic, imagine the issue stated in the context of slavery instead of marriage. What if the question were: "In the resurrection whose slave would a black person be if she or he had belonged successively to seven masters?" And Jesus' answer would be that in heaven the slave and the master would be equal; both would be equal to the angels. There would be no status difference, no distinction in caste. The *slave's* status would be the same as the *master's.*

This pronouncement, this nuance, is what women hear. The woman's status would be equal to the man's status. Both husband and wife would be equal to the angels. The woman would not be a man's appendage, a possession. No doubt this saying seemed as absurd to the listening Sadducees as the idea that Abraham, Isaac and Jacob could already be living in some sort of future life. Jesus in his answer was expanding their thinking—"blowing their minds," we might say.

One common explanation of Jesus' answer is that in the resurrection males won't *need* wives. That is, wives exist only for the purpose of reproducing the male line. In *Interpreter's Bible* (Abingdon, 1951), one commentator notes: "Marriage is an institution necessary for the propagation of the race, but its necessity disappears when men and women become equal to the angels and do not die anymore." Men would not need baby-producing wives nor would women need men. Such a rationale ignores the fact that a question has been asked about a woman who survived seven husbands and that Jesus' answer includes both men and women.

The Sadducees were not really concerned about the woman as a person. They wanted an argument about the resurrection. They wanted to trap Jesus. At theological issue was the belief in an afterlife. In subsequent centuries the discussion of this story has focused on the differences in the Sadducees and the Pharisees and on what Jesus was saying about the resurrection—not on the story's implication for the woman.

Whatever the Sadducees' intent, and in spite of traditional emphases, today women can view the hypothetical story and its tricky question as having some implications for women:

A woman hears about a durable woman who outlived seven husbands.

A woman hears that this person was someone's property—*seven someones*.

A woman hears that this woman was passed from brother to brother, perhaps without her approval, because it was the Deuteronomic law and custom.

A woman understands that not having children would have placed an added stigma on the woman.

A woman hears that Jesus, although he says nothing specific about levirate marriage, disclaims the dependency of the marriage bond in the resurrection.

A woman hears Jesus declaring that she is not someone's property, that she has equal status in the resurrection, that she has a position not relative to anyone else. She is a spiritual being. At least in heaven she will not achieve her identity through someone else.

What sort of person was the woman in the story? First of all the woman was durable. Whether or not the situation was hypothetical, it could have been based on a real-life situation. If she had been married to seven brothers, one might assume that it was not unusual for a woman to outlive her husband, or several husbands. To outlive seven husbands may seem unlikely, but longevity in women, accepted today, may have a longer history than we know about. At least the Sadducees could imagine the situation. It goes without saying that lack of birth control measures and sanitary birth procedures caused many women to die in childbirth. And since better techniques of pre-natal care, delivery and post-natal care have contributed to women's long life expectancy today, this woman's long life was likely related to *not* having children.

Anthropologist Ashley Montague notes in his book *The Natural Superiority of Women* (Collier Books, 1971) that women are less susceptible to thirty or more diseases and inheritable defects than are men, and that aside from muscular strength, women are in most ways more durable. Although no scientific longevity studies exist from the first century, we do know that in some areas the sacrifice of girl babies was commonly practiced. And we can assume that since males were regarded as especially desirable, they probably received preferred treatment. So if some women did outlive men, it may suggest that they had a certain physical durability.

Second, the woman was barren. Whether biologically it was her fault or the husband's fault was not at issue. Barrenness was blamed on the woman. A "barren" woman was much to be pitied, if not despised. She was a failure. One did not speak of a barren or impotent man. Since first-century medical knowledge was limited, it was easy to blame the woman for being barren.

Sterility was considered a trial (Genesis 16:2; 30:2; 1 Samuel 1:5) or a chastisement from God (Genesis 20:18) or a disgrace from which Sarah, Rachel and Leah all tried to clear themselves by adopting the child which their maids bore for their husbands (Genesis 16:2; 30:1-13). In the Code of Hammurabi (about 1700 B.C.) the husband could not take a second wife unless the first was barren. In the region of Kirkuk in the fifteenth century B.C., the barren wife was under an obligation to provide a concubine for her husband.

In Genesis Sarah said to Abraham: "You see the Lord has not allowed me to bear a child. Take my slave girl. Perhaps I shall found a family through her." Both Leah and Rachel offered their slave women to Jacob—and he obligingly "laid with" them and fathered children. Like Sarah, Rachel and Leah, a barren woman felt guilty for the childlessness over which she had no control. Because of it she was considered not OK by society and religion.

If married women were honored chiefly for bearing children, especially sons, then in the case proposed by the Sadducees, for a woman to produce no children in seven marriages made her seven times a failure. One can imagine that each time a brother "took her" as a wife, they hoped for a child. One can imagine the social pressure to which she was subject because of her barren condition. (Today this pressure is not unknown. On Mother's Day, 1974, CBS carried a feature probing the rationale of married couples who choose not to have children. Since most were labeled by family and friends as selfish and insecure and odd, the couples felt obligated to explain their position.)

Third, although the woman was male-controlled, a family

possession, the woman expected this arrangement as her economic and social security (Deuteronomy 25). If a brother would not take his brother's widow to wife, the woman could complain to the elders of the community and even pull off the sandal of the unwilling brother and spit in his face—hinting that sometimes the surviving brother did not take gladly to his levirate obligation. Such a marriage custom put pressure on both sexes to conform, to perpetuate the male line and fortune, and to preserve the ancestral inheritance.

Fourth, as a result of a woman's dependency and her status as possession, the wife position was like an inferior caste. Not only were married women considered to exist for their reproductive function, the Israelite husband was actually called the ba'al or "master" of his wife, just as he was the ba'al of a house or field. According to Proverbs 12:4, a capable wife is "her husband's crown." Indeed, to marry a wife is expressed by the verb ba'al, the root meaning of which is "to become master." Male self-interest suggested that a man have more wives since the husband thereby got another servant.

Marriage, in no uncertain terms, meant submission to a master. The household codes of the New Testament—which were written in the latter third of the first century and later into the second century—reaffirmed the dominance/submission pattern of first century society: masters and slaves, husbands and wives, parents and children. While the early followers of Jesus and the Christian missionary movement practiced an "equality of discipleship" (Fiorenza, p. 251), this caused conflict with the dominant practices of the patriarchal household.

While a few scholars think that the demands for the obedience and submission of wives, children, and slaves are genuinely Christian, the majority see the domestic code as a later Christian adaptation of a Greek/Roman/Jewish code (Fiorenza, p. 254).

From our viewpoint today, it must have been quite surprising to the surrounding society to see the followers of Jesus, and later the followers of Christian missionaries, actually accepting women and slaves as equal participants. Even though later centuries played down the significance of the women friends of Jesus and the women leaders of the early Church, we see Jesus taking up for women and treating them with naturalness and respect—as in this passage about marriage.

The social and legal position of an Israelite wife, however, was inferior to the position of a wife in the great countries round about. In Egypt, notes de Vaux, the wife was often the head of the family, with all the rights such a position entailed. In Babylon she could acquire property, take legal action, and be a party to contracts, and she even had a certain share in her husband's inheritance. Although the Israelite husband could repudiate his wife and she could not claim a divorce, he could not sell her as he could sell his slaves. The wife could not inherit from her husband, nor daughters from their father, except when there was no male heir (Numbers 27:8). All her life the wife remained a minor.

Since first-century culture regarded the Israelite wife as a minor, it is not surprising that Paul and other New Testament writers internalized the concepts of patriarchal marriage and incorporated this view of marriage into instructions about marriage—1 Corinthians 7, 11, and 14; Ephesians 5 and 6; 1 Timothy 2; Colossians 3; 1 Peter 3. (See Katharine M. Rogers, *The Troublesome Helpmate*, pp. 8-11.)

What is surprising is that Jesus seemed to perceive at a greater depth the full humanness of women and treated them with acceptance and respect. In a society where disciples were amazed that Jesus talked with a woman, he obviously knew what the situation of an Israelite wife was. He knew about the levirate law and custom. In the incident with the Sadducees, besides commenting on the resurrection, his surprising answer offered a view in which women and men are regarded with equal consideration. They were to be "equal to the angels." In a future life, then, the religious/cultural conditions of patriarchal life would not exist.

What Jesus says here about women and the wife image is almost incidental to his resurrection comments—and thus has usually been overlooked. Jesus, although he did not address himself directly to a woman's earthly position as a wife, did imply in several places that women are significant human beings in themselves. Never does he denigrate them or limit them. They are not to be relegated to the serving, childbearing role of women in the first century. Five important passages should be noted for their inferences regarding women as wives:

(a) Jesus speaks rather bluntly about the divorce practices of his day. Divorce was a controversial matter because of an on-going debate between two lively rabbinic schools of thought. These were represented by Rabbi Hillel and Rabbi Shammai. Shammai interpreted Deuteronomy 24:1, that a man could divorce a wife for "some unseemly thing in her" (literally in Hebrew, "a matter of indecency"), as having reference only to conjugal infidelity and therefore permitted a husband to divorce his wife only for unfaithfulness. Hillel took the position that any trivial reason which caused a husband displeasure—even putting too much salt into the soup—was sufficient reason for divorce.

Jesus noted that Moses permitted divorce "because of the hardness of your hearts" (Matthew 19:8). Noting that from the beginning of creation this was not so, Jesus asserts that the one flesh concept of marriage should prevail. However, if there is to be a divorce, it should occur only for adultery. In essence this meant that it should be difficult for the husband to divorce the wife—thus giving the woman some security in marriage, some rights. This stance so shocked the disciples that they murmured among themselves, according to the Matthew account, that it is not therefore "expedient to marry."

Although the saying declares that divorced persons who remarry are committing adultery, Bible scholars suggest that this "harsh saying" from Jesus must be taken in the context of his whole attitude of forgiveness and acceptance of all sinners. It seems to express a principle or ideal of marriage, not a legislative enactment. What Jesus was clearly doing was proclaiming that women should have more security in marriage and should not be cast off for Hillel-type petty reasons.

Although divorce was to be limited to adultery, it must be remembered that even adultery was much easier to blame on the woman. The husband was expected to be faithful to his wife, but his infidelity was punished only if he violated the rights of another man by taking a married woman as his accomplice. In contrast with the license which the husband enjoyed, the wife's misconduct was punished severely. Thus Jesus' statement on divorce demands more respect for the wife's position than the culture and religion allowed.

(b) When Jesus tells the story of the woman seeking the lost coin (Luke 15:8-10), he does not reflect on the woman's housekeeping or define her as wife or manager of a home. He elevates the woman's search to represent God seeking the lost, just as the shepherd and the father of the prodigal son also represent God. This woman then, as one God-image in a chapter concerned with the lost, is not restricted to the common role of wife/housekeeper.

(c) In the scriptural reference to the women who followed Jesus (Luke 8:1-3) Luke does not suggest that the women might have neglected their primary duty as wives or mothers. There is no indication that Jesus criticized them or that they were criticized by the Christian community for any wifely neglect or for being part of Jesus' following. They were accepted as followers of Jesus, as disciples, as financial supporters.

(d) In the exchange about the woman who praised the reproductive organs of Mary, we noted that Jesus rejected the view that Mary could be reduced to uterus and breasts, the commonly accepted symbols of the married woman's function, the organs of motherhood. While not denying that function, he avoids praising it and speaks firmly for doing and hearing the will of God—not just giving birth to males who might do God's will. Thus, as Hewitt and Hiatt conclude, Jesus rejected a stereotyped view of woman as homemaker and childbearer (*Women Priests, Yes or No?, op. cit.,* p. 67).

(e) Although Jesus took note of the marital situation of the Samaritan woman at the well, he made no sermonic admonitions concerning her style of life. He treated her as one with whom he could discuss religion, a person to whom he could reveal his messiahship. Again, he does not define the woman as a relative of men, but accepts her as a hearer and messenger of the Word.

Together with the foregoing reference we can place the encounter with the Sadducees in which, although Jesus does not specifically discuss the earthly marriage needs of male or female, he does project a future spiritual existence of both sexes in which the bondage of marriage will have no relevance. Such a stance indicates that, unlike the Sadducees, Jesus *could conceive of* a woman not "belonging" to a husband as the law and social customs dictated. Not only was Jesus' concept incomprehensible to the Sadducees, it has been difficult for subsequent cultures and religions to grant full personhood to women once they become wives.

The biblical one-flesh concept of Genesis 2 and Matthew 19, cited in the traditional marriage service, has been the basis of the married woman's loss of legal rights, loss of her own name, loss of the right to own property, have credit, etc. Leo Kanowitz in his book *Women and the Law,* cites the English jurist Blackstone's description of the doctrine: "By marriage, the husband and wife are one person in law; that is, the very being or legal existence of the woman is suspended during the marriage, or at least is incorporated and consolidated."

This concept has been so generally accepted that only recently has discrimination against married women been resisted and efforts made to change the laws.

We can conclude that in spite of the fact that Jesus does not speak specifically to women as wives, he does offer a mosaic of positive images:

- Woman as an equal in the resurrection, not a possession or a relative.
- Woman as an intellectual/spiritual person with whom he communicated.
- Woman as a God-figure concerned for the lost, not a mere housekeeper.
- Woman as possessing the right to security in marriage, not to be easily cast off as chattel.
- Woman as a follower and financial supporter of his mission.
- Woman as a doer and hearer of the Word, not a reproduction symbol.
- Woman, married or not, as a person to be entrusted with a message.

The composite picture drawn from Jesus' attitude toward the first-century woman is not limited by the culture or religion of his day. Jesus treated women as full human beings, recognized their potential, and took up for them; he saw that as wives they were taken advantage of; and in divorce and levirate marriage he saw them treated as birth vessels and property. He deliberately chose to reveal himself to women as the Messiah and the resurrected Lord. He was a compassionate person who saw human beings rather than labels or categories.

And he expected women to be active and to lead others in the Christian community. He incorporated women into his close circle of friends and disciples and into his ministry. Jesus' view was indeed liberated for his day—and prophetic for ours.

JESUS AND THE
CRITICAL SISTERS

Luke 10:38-42; Mark 12:18-27

Jesus, it appears, acted especially human around women, evoking their frankness and intimacy in response.

Consider two familiar stories about Mary and Martha. In one, Martha is preparing food in the kitchen and wants Mary to help her. Jesus rebukes Martha as being too busy and says that Mary has "chosen the better thing"—that is, listening and talking with him in the other room. In the other story, Lazarus has died and both of his sisters complain to Jesus, "If you had been here our brother would not have died."

The stories are unrelated and are told in two different Gospels. What they have in common is the relationship displayed between Jesus and Martha and Mary. If these friends had not had a certain depth of relationship, Martha would not have felt free to complain about Mary's lack of assistance. And when Lazarus died, had the sisters not been intimate friends of Jesus, they would not have freely complained to Jesus about what they felt to be his negligence in their brother's death.

Martha and Mary, living at Bethany near Jerusalem, had such a special closeness with Jesus that they could complain to him in a normal way. They knew Jesus so well that they believed he could have healed their brother. As close to Jesus as sisters, as close as old friends who could be frank to one another, they said what they thought. Because Jesus stayed frequently in their home they were familiar with one another's habits, language, ways of communicating—as well as the content of Jesus' preaching and teaching. And Jesus, for his part, knew their personalities, their style of life, including the usual assignment of household jobs.

Only in such a friendly shared relationship could these two women have felt free enough to be critical of Jesus.

Early Christians knew that Jesus was truly human—as well as God's chosen. In nineteen centuries, however, tradition has so deified Jesus that even when we see him acting especially human in the Gospel stories, we tend to ignore it or explain away this humanness—and to explain away his close friends' quite human treatment of him. Many questions have arisen, for example, concerning the story about the death of Lazarus, because of Jesus' weeping. How could such grief be reconciled with the divinity of Jesus? To disallow grief or anger or love in Jesus is to disallow humanness.

Yet here are two women who treat Jesus in a human, pressuring fashion, to which he responds in kind. "Why don't you make Mary help me?" Martha complains. And later: "If you had been here, Lazarus would not have died." What could be more honest and sharing between loving, trusting people?

First, these stories tell us something about the relationship between Mary and Martha as sisters, as well as the relationship between Jesus and the two women. Second, the stories have implications concerning assigned roles in home and church and society. Third, they contain implications about the conflict between doing and being, or between the serving life and the intellectual life.

In the first account Martha was conscious of her household duty as a hostess. Was it not obvious that Jesus should be fed as a special guest? But Mary was more concerned to visit and talk with Jesus. "Lord, do you not care that my sister has left me to serve alone? Tell her then to help me." The relationship between the sisters is deeply involved in this confrontation. The very fact that Martha urges Jesus to tell Mary to help her suggests a pattern of customary activity—that Mary usually

does help. If Martha always cooked and Mary always enter-
tained a guest (rigid assignment of roles) there would have
been no problem. To say to Jesus, "Make her come to help,"
implies: "This is where she belongs."

Both of these women are self-confident. Martha knows
she is right, managing the work in the kitchen. She knows what
should be served and how to go about preparing it. Mary, too, is
self-confident. Even if she often helps in the kitchen, she knows
where she wants to be—in the other room with Jesus, talking,
sharing, learning, discussing religion. Since Jewish women
were not allowed to learn the Torah, for Jesus to discuss
religion with women was perceived as a special opportunity.
(Remember in another story the passage, "The disciples mar-
veled that he was talking with a woman.") Mary was willing to
grasp that opportunity even if it offended her sister.

Sibling rivalry, to use a modern term, seems to be an
element in the conflict. Since Mary, Martha, and Lazarus lived
together, the question of who does what in the home was part
of the problem of living. Where three adults resided, we cannot assume that a patriarchal pattern of role assignment pre-
vailed. Although neither woman seems to have a business or
any sign of visible income, we might assume that there was
some inheritance. If the home belonged to Martha as some
have suggested, she might have been a widow who, unlike the
usual condition of widows under Jewish inheritance laws, did
have some property. Or property could have been inherited by
Lazarus.

The fact that Martha appeals to Jesus to take sides indicates rivalry. If there were none she could have said, "Mary,
come and help me." But she felt that Mary needed extra
persuasion. Jesus, like a parent, should "make" Mary do her
duty—that is, her duty as Martha sees it.

Perhaps Jesus had mediated a dispute between the sisters
before. Their rivalry dated from childhood, one sister being
more outgoing, active and managing, the other more intro-

spective and articulate. Mary may have been more of a student, eager to pick up learning from rabbis and teachers, the learning that Jewish women were denied. Martha may have been the elder sister, responsible for household tasks, a natural organizer. In spite of normal tensions between them, the sisters were close to Jesus.

Aside from the relationship between the sisters, what was the relationship between Jesus and Martha and Mary like? From our viewpoint today the sisters were liberated in regard to community standards—a remarkable and unnoticed element in the story. They were openly entertaining a well-known man in their home. Jesus was an accepted friend of the family, accepted by them and by the community.

"Now Jesus loved Martha and her sister and Lazarus," comments John 11:5. What sort of love? Could there indeed have been sexual jealousy between the sisters for the attention of Jesus? Or was it platonic, a friendly relationship? As lively, physical human beings, we cannot discount the possibility that there was more than friendly interaction among the three, a factor which could have entered into the resentment Martha expresses. Attracted to Jesus, she wanted to be in his presence too. Yet at the same time she wanted to please him by preparing food.

Whether Jesus was father figure, brother figure, possible love object or merely dear friend, we do not know; we can only speculate. Whatever the type, there is no doubt that the relationship with Jesus was close and dynamic.

In the second story, reported in the fourth Gospel, the close and critical relationship prevails. After Lazarus died, the sisters were being consoled by many of their Jewish friends. Martha, upon hearing that Jesus is approaching Bethany, goes out to meet him and complains at once, "Lord, if you had been here, my brother would not have died." She adds a hopeful comment which shows her profound understanding of Jesus.

"And even now I know that whatever you ask from God, God will give you."

Jesus tells Martha that her brother will rise. She responds that she knows he will rise in the resurrection. Then Jesus says to her, " I am the resurrection and the life; he who believes in me, though he die, yet shall he live, and whoever lives and believes in me shall never die. Do you believe this?" She said to him, "Yes, Lord; I believe that you are the Christ, the Son of God, he who is coming into the world."

Note: Jesus and a woman are discussing *who he is*.

It is extremely interesting and important that it is Martha, the domestic-type Martha, who is given this speech by the writer of the fourth Gospel. We might have expected it from the mouth of Mary, the spiritual-type Mary, had we stereotyped the sisters based solely on the Luke story.

Next, Mary, rising from where she was sitting in the house being consoled by friends, goes out to speak with Jesus. She falls at his feet and says also, "Lord, if you had been here, my brother would not have died." Jesus is moved and troubled in spirit. He weeps and is led to the cave where Lazarus is buried. When he asks that the stone be removed from the grave, the practical Martha speaks up bluntly, "Lord, by this time there will be an odor, for he has been dead four days."

Again, a human reaction, Martha is skeptical. Had Martha been less sure of herself in relation to Jesus she would hardly have offered resistance at this point. Rather than rejoice that her brother might soon emerge alive, she offers her healthy skepticism. Again she shows a freedom of thought based on a solid relationship—and based also on faith, for we remember how she said earlier that whatever Jesus asked of God, God would grant.

In both of these incidents, then, an intimate relationship among Mary, Martha and Jesus is indicated. Both sisters speak freely of their feelings and thoughts, and Jesus responds frankly to them. Martha, as well as Mary, discusses religion with Jesus. Amazingly, the conversation with Martha is spelled out in the fourth Gospel, not the one with Mary in Luke, proving Martha's depth and spiritual understanding. In both instances Jesus willingly treated women as full intellectual human beings, persons who could be learners, knowledgeable and articulate, persons who could believe and explain that belief to others.

The second issue to be considered is that, based on the Luke story by itself, Mary and Martha have traditionally symbolized a polarization of women's roles. Dorothy Sayers says she has never heard a sermon preached on the story of Martha and Mary that did not attempt to explain away its text. Why? Because we could not get on without Martha. She was doing "a really feminine job, whereas Mary was just behaving like any other disciple, male or female; and that is a hard pill to swallow" (*Are Women Human?*, Inter-Varsity Press, 1971, pp. 46-47).

Whenever Martha and Mary are posed as representative of women's roles, Mary becomes a shining example and Martha a whining example. Martha is presented as a busybody, a complaining housewife, obsessed with preparing a gourmet meal, ignorant of the importance of the guest in the home. And Mary, in contrast, has been elevated as the ideal spiritual woman, somehow liberated from the domestic role to be with Jesus, the "better thing." The kitchen tasks do not weigh on her mind as they do on Martha's.

Such a traditional interpretation does not do justice to the story. It ignores certain vibrations. Martha is not happy in doing the tasks in the kitchen. She complains because she must cook by herself. She wants help. And as she and Mary both know, the food preparation must be done, but Martha, like many women, *resents being saddled with the chore alone.*

Many women feel great identity with Martha. In the kitchen is exactly where society and the church have put women.

"Traditionally in America," says Beulah Larson, "the women of the church have been segregated into auxiliaries, boxed into a Martha role of housekeeping and hospitality, while unheeded go the words of Jesus, 'Mary has chosen the right thing and it shall not be taken away from her'" (*Women, a Questioning of Past and Present,* The American Lutheran Church, 1972).

But—*it has been taken away from her.* Bible interpreters and preachers may criticize those who are distracted with much serving, yet the church has seen to it that women have no other function than that of serving. Women tend the kitchen, women run the Sunday schools, visit the sick, clean the altarware and provide fund-raising suppers.

In the story Martha complains bluntly—and many women hear her clearly. Jesus, by faulting Martha, makes her feel even worse. She was trying to please him, yet here he is siding with her sister, saying, "Don't overdo in the kitchen, Martha. Food doesn't have to be extravagant in appearance or preparation. Come on in here with Mary and me."

Martha felt put down. This job is not more her job than it is Mary's. If both women served in the kitchen, then both could be learning from Jesus and enjoying his company. Martha indicates an unresolved hostility. Women hear her saying: *I feel angry, Jesus. Not everybody can be spiritual all the time. If someone sits by you and talks, then someone else has to bake the bread and cook the fish.*

At least, Martha is expressing her emotions. Miller observes in *Toward a New Psychology of Women* (p. 39) that women have been so encouraged to concentrate on the feelings and responses of others that they have been diverted from examining their own, from really *knowing themselves.* Martha shows here that she not only knows how she feels—resentful to have kitchen work dumped on her—but she feels free enough with Jesus to say so.

Martha is doing work that is necessary, but her sister and Jesus do not see the value of what she is doing. To her, she is serving and her sister is goofing off. She resents Jesus' elevating what Mary is doing and putting down what she is doing. He seems to be more concerned about food for the mind and spirit than about food for the body. Martha knows that at other times Jesus *was* concerned about food, feeding the multitude, providing wine at the Cana wedding. Martha's own integrity won't let her do what Mary is doing. Her *duty* in the kitchen comes before her *desire* to be with Jesus. *This need* comes before *that need.*

Martha embodies the dilemma of all women. Many women feel that there is hypocrisy inherent in the traditional interpretation of this story. From a woman's point of view, Jesus is being unfair. Women are burdened unfairly with serving in the home, the church, and society's institutions—and then are blamed with being too concerned with that function.

It is a no-win position. If women are sensitive, they ask: Which need comes first? By accepting the Martha role, they get blamed by Jesus and the church for being too busy-busy. If they prefer being Marys, they nevertheless have to perform Martha jobs.

More and more women today are declaring a self-identity that could be compared to Mary's—independent, seeking, learning, self-affirming, interested in theology. Throughout Christian history, women who have been Marys have had to achieve under great handicaps. Many potential Marys have been lost to Christianity because of a lack of encouragement or opportunity. In the Catholic traditon, in order to be a "Mary" a woman had to give up family life and become a mystic or a sister of an order. (See Mary Daly, *The Church and the Second Sex,* for her discussion of women such as Mary Ward, who was persecuted and repressed by papal authorities.)

In Protestant tradition there have been few women spiritual/intellectual leaders—no women Luthers or Augustines, no female Barths or Bonhoeffers. However today the scene is changing. There are thousands of women studying theology in seminaries, feminist theorists writing about their explorations and lecturing to wide audiences. We have people like Mary Daly who in *Beyond God the Father* asked us to take a critical look at theology, and like Fiorenza who in *In Memory of Her* asks us to take a critical look at the Bible and its contexts. Like Phyllis Trible, Letty Russell, and other feminist theologians, these explorers of mind and history accept the observation that all texts are products of an androcentric patriarchal culture and history.

What we are in the midst of is a mind-quake that is so dramatic that we have no idea yet of the dimensions of it. Not only the assumptions of traditional theology but the very structures of organized patriarchal Christianity are being challenged. As Nancy Hardesty comments in a review of Fiorenza's book (*Daughters of Sarah*, July/August 1985 p. 9): "Whether we read these books or not, the church's self-understanding can never be the same again because of them."

In society as well as the church, Martha is the projected image for women. Women's magazines, run by male staffs, have encouraged the modern woman to be an expert Martha, a buyer, decorator, gourmet cook—"busy about many things." Her socialization through school texts, her image in the media, the expectations she is fed by family, friends, and teachers—all is directed toward achievement in the domestic realm.

John K. Galbraith noted in his previously cited article that women are manipulated by the economy, used as buyers of products without whom the market could not function. To motivate buying, industry exacerbates women's feelings of inadequacy (their floors aren't shiny enough, their bras aren't the correct model, their laxatives too harsh, their coffee not rich enough, etc.). As Betty Friedan pointed out, in order to respond to the constant pressure to buy products and to conform to society's expectations, women have "expanded housewifery to fill the day" (*Feminine Mystique*, Norton, 1963).

When this sort of Martha woman is told that Mary—a person she dare not be and has few models for—has chosen the better part, she feels incensed and trapped. Many modern women want support and approval for what they have become—with the church's and society's blessing. They want to know that it is OK to be a Martha.

If, on the other hand, they have secretly felt like a Mary, but have been rebuffed in attempts to avoid the Martha role and be like Mary, they are equally confused. Recently a woman said to me, "I have always wanted to be a Mary—but I thought that would be selfish." Women's socialization is ironic and laced with hypocrisy. While boys and men learn that to be achievers is right and expected of them, girls and women learn that to achieve in a vocational sense (other than nurse or teacher) is somehow regarded as selfish; *their* obligation is to serve the family.

Women, then, are receiving a mixture of signals both from society and from the church. Society tells them to be home-makers, but considers it "not working." The church tells them to be servants—but offers this Luke story charging the serving Martha with being too "busy about many things."

No wonder many women are angry and confused.

A third way to look at the Luke story of Mary and Martha is to present it as showing the polarity between *doing* and *being*, or between the serving life and the intellectual life. The trouble with this view is that it seems inconsistent with Jesus' negative attitude toward the intellectual Pharisees, on the one hand, and his emphasis on serving the "least of these my brethren" in Matthew 25.

In their previously cited *The Mission and Message of Jesus*, Major, Manson and Wright note: "This incident has been used to stress the superiority of the life of religious contemplation over that of practical activity, but if that practical activity be devotion to the service of others, even though it be only directed to the relief of their physical needs, it has much to justify it in the teaching of Jesus. The Christian religion, in contrast to Buddhism, is essentially a life of practical service inspired by divine love rather than a life of mystical contemplation" (p. 280).

If Martha symbolizes the traditional woman's position—tending, serving, nurturing—then Mary symbolizes the usual male position—disciple, leader, apostle, theologian.

In discussing this story Leonard Swidler says, "It is difficult to imagine how Jesus could possibly have been clearer in his insistence that women were called to the intellectual life, the spiritual life, just as were men" ("Jesus Was a Feminist," *art. cit.*).

According to this activist vs. intellectual view, women do what comes "naturally," thus freeing men to study theology, run the church and other institutions. Women serve—and men lead. Martha conveniently frees Mary to be at Jesus' feet. Of course this sort of distinction need not be restricted to a sex-role perspective. Within a certain vocation or profession such as the ministry, there can be the same conflict. Should a minister or priest be an activist or one who studies, does theology and concentrates on the preaching or interpretation of the Word?

Rather than offering dichotomies, perhaps the two stories of Jesus and the critical sisters could provide a model for modern Christians. In a profound way the combined stories demonstrate *wholeness* in a complex relationship. Jesus and Mary and Martha treated each other as persons rather than assigning each other to limited functions and stereotypes. (The sisters' struggle over function in the Luke story indicates their healthy refusal to be limited.) Both sexes were honest and caring. Jesus was frank with both sisters, and they in turn treated him with openness. He plainly discussed his teachings and thinking with both Mary and Martha. They in turn show evidence of their understanding.

To demonstrate wholeness, Martha and Mary should not represent either-or possibilities, but the variety of human personhood in relation to Jesus. Each person, rather than limited to one function, can be not only a serving person, but one who shares the "better part" with Jesus.

Today we know that both women and men are spiritual and intellectual, that both are capable of teaching, serving, witnessing, leading and being creative. We know that no characteristics belong exclusively to one sex. To discover afresh the humanness of all women and men will be not only liberating to individuals, but enriching to the church.

Actually, in their way, Martha and Mary were feminists. By her complaint in the Luke story, Martha wanted freedom from drudgery. By her eagerness to share her mind with Jesus, Mary wanted freedom for theology. Like both of these critical, freely-relating women, women today can combine both purposes in their search for wholeness.

JESUS AND THE
WOMEN PREACHERS

John 4:4-42; Luke 24:1-24

To "go and tell" is to preach the Gospel. At two crucial and dramatic points Jesus chose women for his own self-revelation and sent them to spread the Word, to preach the Gospel.

The first woman who "goes and tells" is the woman at the well. By first-century social customs it is amazing that Jesus readily discussed religion at a chance meeting with a woman. It suggests his readiness to accept an average person as an intelligent human being. Beyond that, this woman of Samaria is the first person to receive the message that Jesus is the expected one, the Messiah. Jesus discusses spiritual matters with her, explaining that he has "living water" to offer, and then reveals to her that he is the Messiah.

What does the woman do? She goes to the people in the nearby city and tells them what she has heard. Her response to Jesus is a sense of mission resulting in action. And the people's response to her preaching is action. They not only come to hear Jesus, but many believe. Her preaching is effective. It gets results.

The second crucial drama is after the resurrection. Women dominate the scene. They are not only the first witnesses to the fact that the tomb is empty, but they are the first persons to whom the Lord reveals himself. On top of that, they are the first persons he sends forth with a message. On this occasion women exemplify two ways in which people can be witnesses. The women are the first witnesses *to* the event. And they are witnesses in the sense of going and telling *about* the event.

Thus women were the first to preach the resurrection even to the disciples—or to anyone. Not only did a woman proclaim *Jesus as Messiah,* but women were the first to preach *Jesus as risen.*

Why did Jesus rely on women to be his first messengers, to be receivers of two earth-shaking revelations? Why have they not been credited by traditional Christian interpretation as proclaimers, messengers, witnesses, preachers? Why have these absolutely stunning breakthroughs for women not been perceived as breakthroughs?

It can hardly be over-emphasized that women as mouth-pieces, women as witnesses, women as preachers, as God's vessels of proclamation, have been virtually ignored in Christian history, while women as birth vessels or virgins have been emphasized to the point of stereotype. Now we suddenly see that the woman who proclaimed Jesus' messiahship while he lived, and the women who proclaimed his risenness after the crucifixion, have been underestimated.

Christianity has not explored the question: *Why did Jesus choose women first as the media for these messages rather than his male apostles?* And why has the significance of his choices been ignored, covered up, or shrugged off for centuries? Why, especially, did Paul in his famous listing of post-resurrection appearances of Jesus in 1 Corinthians 15 not even mention the appearance of Jesus to the women?

How did Jesus see these women? Did Jesus see persons there where Christian tradition has seen only stereotypes? With no fanfare Jesus broke through images of women current in first-century culture and religion. Was it accidental? I suggest that there might be reasons why Jesus honored women by choosing them for these functions.

First, the woman at the well. This woman was not just any woman. To begin with, she had three strikes against her. She had a low assigned status *as a woman* in the culture and religion of the first century. She had a low assigned status *as a Samaritan*—a kindred people whom the Jews despised. She had a third low status as a woman *whose life-style was suspect.*

How can we explain that Jesus chose for his critical message to the community such a negative-value person? A woman, a Samaritan, a sinner. It is easy to see that because these three negatives are frequently so entrancing to the preacher or interpreter it is difficult to get past them to see the woman as a person.

Traditionally, sermons about the woman at the well emphasize that she was a Samaritan woman who had had five husbands and was living with a man not her husband. *Living in sin.* This point makes such a fine jumping-off place for the judgmental bias in Christianity for sexual sins—especially as they are evidenced by women—that the sermon often becomes one about sexual sins. One wonders if preachers have ever faulted the five husbands—or the man with whom the woman was living. Indeed, John Calvin in his *Commentaries* readily lays a heavy sin trip on the woman by speculating that the woman was such a "forward and disobedient wife that she constrained her husbands to divorce her, that she did not cease to sin and prostituted herself to fornication." In contrast to such prejudice, apparently the six men enjoyed a position similar to the male partner of the "woman caught in adultery"—neither pursued nor blamed.

Thus, sexual sin can easily become the point of emphasis, not why Jesus chose the woman for his attention, how she responded, the content of their discussion—and how Christians should regard the woman and label her.

The careful Bible student notices that only three verses out of thirty are devoted to the marital status of the woman.

The other verses concern her religious discussion with Jesus, her excited action as a result of receiving Jesus' blockbuster message, and the effect of her preaching on the people in her city.

It is exciting to see how the themes of faith and revelation dominate the dramatic narrative. The woman has an intellectual and theological curiosity. Fiorenza notes the progression of the statements: Jew (v. 9), Lord (v. 11), greater than our father Jacob (v. 12), prophet (v.19), salvation comes from the Jews (v. 22), Messiah (v. 25), I am (v. 26), the Christ (vv. 25, 26), Savior of the world (v. 42). The animated discussion also concerns the content of worship and the meaning of "living water" (Fiorenza, p. 328).

There are three scenes to the story. In the *first scene* Jesus asks for a drink. It is a simple act, one which shows his humanness (which the Gnostics were prone to deny). Significant also is the fact that *Jesus is asking a woman to minister to his need.* He is thirsty. He asks the help of a woman.

In this scene the woman and Jesus engage in six exchanges. "How is it that you, a Jew, ask a drink of me, a woman of Samaria?" She has cause to wonder. Not only did the Jews not associate with the Samaritans, they despised them. When Jesus says he has "living water" to give, the woman retorts: "You have nothing to draw with. Where do you get that water? Are you greater than our father Jacob who gave us this well?"

At once we see a woman who is quite independent, not easily pressed into service or conformity by a stranger. She knows the heritage of her people who descended from Jacob, who based their religion on the Pentateuch.

When at this point Jesus asks her to call her husband and she acknowledges that she has no husband, Jesus remarks that she has been married five times and is now living with a man not her husband. There is, however, no pursuit at all of this subject; the two people return to discussing religion, specifically worship. Where to worship was a thorny issue between Jews and Samaritans. "You worship what you do not know. We worship what we know, for salvation is from the Jews," says Jesus. The woman, acknowledging him as a prophet, shows her learning by saying that she knows the Messiah is coming who is called Christ, "who will show us all things."

The climax of the interchange is Jesus' self-revelation: " I who speak to you am he."

In this first dramatic scene we observe a lively communication. The woman speaks up to Jesus. Although she does not initially respond to the request for a drink, Scripture does not give support to those interpreters who claim that she is rude, that she jeers and scoffs at him, that she insults Jesus. She is merely discussing issues with him; we do not know her tone. To be sure, she is skeptical, perhaps amused as she points out that Jews don't usually speak to Samaritans and that he has nothing to draw water with. Are we to fault her because she is sharp and has a ready answer for a Jewish stranger?

She is not only responsive to what Jesus says, immediately asking for "this water" he claims to have, but she is open to the idea that this water is special. The woman is intelligent and well informed about the issues dividing Samaritans and Jews. She knows a Messiah is expected and she recognizes Jesus as a prophet. Already we see a person who is responsive to verbal exchange, sharp, skeptical, quick to see meaning—and a person who is open to Jesus' self-declaration.

In *scene two,* the disciples come up and marvel that Jesus is talking with a woman. There was a rabbinical saying, "A man should hold no conversation with a woman in the street, not even with his own wife, still less with any other woman, lest *men should gossip*" (emphasis added). Today such a sexist attitude seems shocking indeed—but it indicates the low status of women in the first century. In this case, the woman is irrepressible and pays the disciples no mind.

She is so motivated with her new insight and information

that she goes into the nearby city saying to the people, "Come and see a man who told me all that I ever did. . . . Is this not the Christ?" John notes that many Samaritans from that city "believed in him *because of the woman's testimony*" (emphasis added).

Jesus gave the woman a message bombshell. He knew it would motivate her to preach. It acted as a spiritual "call" within her. She went forth immediately to tell a message —and the message got through. *She was the medium.* She left her water pot to go and tell. She left her woman-job for her preacher-job. Her culturally assigned status gave way to her Jesus-assigned status—one who is worthy to go and tell.

In his *Commentaries,* John Calvin acknowledges that her "earnestness and promptitude" are worthy of attention, "for scarcely had she tasted Christ when she spread his fame throughout the whole city." And he adds, "She merely does the office of a trumpet or a bell to invite others to come to Christ." Merely?

That is true preaching.

The fourth Gospel records a further development. The people in the city were so moved that they asked Jesus to stay with them, and "he stayed there two days. And many more believed." Although Paul is credited with expanding the Gospel to all people, not just Jews, here we have an instance of Jesus—because of a woman's preaching—going and staying with Samaritans in their city for two days.

The *third scene* of the story dramatizes the belief of the people. They make a point of telling the woman preacher: "It is no longer because of your words that we believe, for we have heard for ourselves, and we know that this is indeed the Savior of the world." Again, there is recognition of her preaching—and perhaps a bit of a put-down, a reluctance to acknowledge that *she* brought the message, a reluctance to give her due credit. One commentator in *Interpreter's Bible (op. cit.)* reflects this bias by saying she was a "most unlikely person to bring any authentic tidings, but she impressed them enough" that they came to hear Jesus.

Calvin can't resist saying in his *Commentaries* that the Samaritans "appear to boast that they have now a stronger foundation than a woman's tongue, which is, for the most part, light and trivial." Again, evidence of the bad press women have had.

Despite the fact that the sexist blinders of centuries have put down the woman, this story is an important breakthrough for women. Here is Jesus' longest conversation with a woman. Obviously when the fourth Gospel reconstructs such a conversation from the oral tradition, we must make allowances for the restructuring of the conversation. Yet it is probable that many persons had heard about this confrontation, and that the oral tradition was well known in the area.

To sum up the main content of the story, Jesus is saying to the woman: (1) salvation is from the Jews; (2) God is spirit; (3) he himself is the expected one, the Messiah. Jesus confidently gives his explosive message to a person who carries it immediately, vividly and effectively to a nearby audience.

How shall we perceive this bright and aggressive woman? What shall we say of the fact that Jesus chose her as his agent?

Did Jesus deliberately give the honor of his self-revelation to a woman, or was the woman at the well merely the first person at hand when he deemed it right to reveal himself to people as the Messiah? It is difficult to conclude that Jesus' choice of a person was accidental. Surely he had some purpose in choosing the woman as his mouthpiece, as his first messenger, his spokesperson.

Would it not have been more logical for Jesus to divulge this message to some trusted and respected male Jew of upright character and marital status? Why not to one of his select apostles? Why not to one of the scribes or Pharisees? Although Jesus did not gravitate toward the educated elite, males *were* the honored people in the community. Why would he select someone who was not only an offense to the Jews, an outsider, a woman, but also someone whose personal life was easily criticized?

Could it be possible that Jesus saw this woman as one whom people would listen to precisely because she was different? Did he respond to her intelligence with a sense of expectation and confidence? Did he think of women as goers and doers, as convincing and articulate communicators? As more enthusiastic when they had a loaded message? Did Jesus appraise this woman as a dynamic person who would make an impact on others? Certainly a male Jew of Galilee or Judea would hardly have had entree with the Samaritans in their own city. And further—perhaps a woman who already in community eyes had broken with standards of propriety was one who had nothing to lose by being outspoken. Why should the people not listen to her?

Could it be that Jesus had another motive, that he deliberately chose a woman to disperse some of the strictures he saw placed on women? Could he have intended to elevate the position of women, to identify them as OK preachers, and the patriarchal world of that day—and since— simply did not get the message?

Perhaps Jesus intended to show that although salvation was from the Jews, she who was a Samaritan could be a preacher of the message. As with the woman at Simon's house, he could have intended to show that a person's marital history or even state of "living in sin" was not a barrier to spreading the Gospel.

Jesus may have looked through the three negatives— woman, Samaritan, sinner— and seen a *person useful for the kingdom.*

Although we can't see inside Jesus' mind, we can see the three images of women that are involved in the story, and we can see that Jesus broke through these limitations imposed by culture and religion on the women of the first century.

There is a further aspect to the story which ties it in with the drama of the women after the resurrection. Women in Judaism were not recognized as valid witnesses. In honoring the woman at the well as well as the women after the resurrection, Jesus broke through this barrier to motivate women to be his first messengers/witnesses.

Consider the resurrection women. It is well known that women were honored as the first witnesses to the empty tomb and were the first persons to see the risen Lord. But several implications have not been examined by traditional interpreters.

Why did Jesus reveal his risenness to women? Was their selection as the first witnesses and preachers merely happenstance? Or did Jesus deliberately choose women for a purpose? If women were chosen for this mission, what meaning does it have for lives of women today? What significance can it have for the church as it struggles to accept women as equal human beings in practice as well as in theory and theology?

Christians have traditionally been subjected to a lack of insight—or a coverup—of these significant issues. Why especially did Paul ignore these women-related events?

According to the Gospel story, the disciples had fled the scene at the crucifixion. It was the women who stayed faithful. This fact has hardly been mentioned in centuries of preaching about these events. What does it prove about the chosen—then numbering eleven—that they fled the responsibility of the cross during the final hours? What does it prove about the faithfulness of women, the loyalty and depth of their devotion, that they remained by Jesus, no matter what the dangers? Alas, male preachers, Bible scholars and theologians have made little of this defection of men and the faithfulness of the women.

Although they vary, at least the Gospel writers give credit to the women for coming to the tomb on the third day to minister to Jesus' body. The accounts tell what the women saw and what they did. Mark credits Mary Magdalene, Mary the mother of James, and Salome with coming to bring spices to anoint Jesus' body. "Other sources" credit Mary Magdalene with seeing the risen Lord, who then went and told those who had been with him, but they would not believe it.

Luke reports that Mary Magdalene, Joanna, Mary the mother of James and other women heard the message from two men in dazzling apparel. They told what they had seen and heard to "the eleven and to all the rest"—but these words "seemed to them an idle tale and they did not believe them."

Matthew names Mary Magdalene and the other Mary as the witnesses who received the message from "an angel of the Lord." The angel instructs the women to go quickly and tell the disciples that Jesus has risen, that "he is going before you to Galilee, there you will see him." Jesus himself meets the women and says, "Go and tell my brethren to go to Galilee and there they will see me."

So, in the Synoptics, there is no doubt that the women are given specific instructions to go and tell—and indeed are instructed as to the content of their message. In the fourth Gospel it is Mary Magdalene who reports to Peter about the stone rolled away. "They have taken the Lord out of the tomb, and we do not know where they have laid him." After Peter sees for himself and tells the other disciples, they go back to their homes. But Mary stays near the tomb.

There follows the familiar story of Jesus communicating with Mary and telling her to inform the brethren that he is ascending to the Father. She tells the disciples "I have seen the Lord" and reports what he had said to her.

The Gospel accounts are explicit. Paul, however, in his 1 Corinthians 15 listing of the post-resurrection appearances of Jesus, does not mention the appearance to the women. Paul acts as if the appearance did not happen. Although Bible scholars agree that 1 Corinthians pre-dates the Gospels, what can be the explanation of Paul's omission?

Dr. John Knox, a scholar and authority on Paul and his writings, has two suggestions as to why Paul omits the appearance to the women. First, perhaps Paul was not familiar with that particular tradition, a somewhat shaky explanation since Paul was a contemporary of Luke's. Or perhaps, suggests Knox, Paul did not want the record to stand on the questionable witness of women. Paul was, of course, a man of his times, educated in the elitist Jewish manner, reflecting at many points a first-century patriarchal socialization in regard to women.

In spite of Paul's omission, Christian tradition has given great emphasis to the women at the tomb and the appearance of Jesus to the women—especially at Easter time. What it has not done, however, is to credit them, to label them, as proclaimers of the Gospel, as the *first preachers sent forth by the risen Lord* to tell others what happened

Had early Christians seen the women in this light, perhaps women would have been accepted as ministers and priests during the long centuries of their exclusion from the Christian ministry.

Why were the women not perceived as proclaimers, as preachers, as witnesses to the Word? Was it because the Jews did not accept the witness of women as valid? Was it because it was a one-event action and the women did not continue their message-bearing? Perhaps all these reasons entered in—but chiefly the latter.

Women are seen as gossips. Women go and tell their neighbors. Women are talkative. Calvin provides an example of this perception in his discussion of the Samaritan woman. Jesus brought up the subject of the woman's husbands, he suggests in his *Commentaries,* "in order to repress the woman's talkativeness." Rather than perceiving two people discussing religion, Calvin saw a woman being "talkative" to Jesus.

We expect women to get excited about dramatic happenings. Women, we say, are emotional, are concerned about relationships with people. These are women categories. When men do the same things, they are seen as active and aggressive. They are labeled differently. For instance, Scripture says that Peter and the other disciple ran to the tomb and that "the other disciple outran Peter." No one points out that this is an emotional, excited reaction. When women show excitement they are *noticed* as emotional or hysterical. Men are called "active" or "assertive" or "dynamic." Our perception differs frequently according to the sex of the perceived person.

Thus when women go forth and tell, proclaim a message, preach about their experiences as witnesses to a great event, they are seen through cultural stereotypes. In this way our customary social formulations about women have blinded us to the perception of them as preachers, witnesses and doers of the Word.

Racism provides a good comparison. Racism and sexism are similar in their cultural patterns of stereotyping persons and roles. If one has only seen blacks as servants, porters, housemaids, or athletes, one finds it difficult to acknowledge a black judge, a black physician or a Martin Luther King. One does not have a convenient category for such a person. TV character Archie Bunker illustrates the principle. When Archie meets a black doctor in the elevator, he tries to relate to him on the man's low assigned status level as a black, not on his achievement level as a doctor. Archie's doctor category permits only whites.

Thus with women until recently, most people have had minister/priest categories which permit only males. Even if women are performing the acts of a minister or proclaimer, they are not so recognized or labeled. The average person may not have a mental category for women as Ph.D's, as physicians or attorneys, as Nobel Prize winners, as bank presidents. If women are denied by culture and religion a certain label or acceptance in a role or job, the tendency of people in that culture and religion is to ignore them in that capacity or to call it something else. (Men are also subject to this sort of prejudice. Male nurses report a kind of ostracism practiced by women nurses.)

To summarize, on these two important occasions when Jesus chose to use women as his medium, as his messengers, their performance was treated as if it were just an activity women do—gossips, non-valid witness, hysterical—not as if they were breaking through role assignments, cultural conditions, not as if Jesus wanted them to be seen in a new light.

Today we are removing our sexist blinders and are able to see that Jesus inspired and sent forth women as his chosen tellers of the message. Women, we now perceive, were the first preachers of the Good News: *He is risen!*

If Christian churches today can begin to perceive women in this new light, revealed as messengers and preachers chosen for the function by Jesus himself, the options for women are broadened. This insight shows that the struggle for women's equality and liberation is grounded in Jesus' life and the resurrection event.

Jesus knew what he was doing. He affirmed women in ways his contemporaries and later followers did not recognize. What this view offers is a new insight—a new perception of a reality of wholeness which was there all the time.

BIBLIOGRAPHY

Beach, Diane Lee, "Fun with Dick and Jane," *Spectrum/ International Journal of Religious Education,* Sept./Oct. 1971.

Calvin, John, *Commentary on the Gospel According to John,* translated from Latin by the Rev. William Pringle, Vol. 1, Wm. B. Eerdmans Publishing Co., Grand Rapids, MI., 1949.

Carlisle, Thomas John, *Eve and After,* Wm. B. Eerdmans, Grand Rapids, 1984.

Daly, Mary, *The Church and the Second Sex,* Harper and Row, New York and Evanston, 1968.

_____*Beyond God the Father,* Beacon Press, Boston, 1973.

De Vaux, Roland, *Ancient Israel, Its Life and Institutions,* McGraw-Hill Book Co. Inc., New York, 1965.

Doely, Sarah Bentley (ed.), *Women's Liberation and the Church,* Association Press, New York, 1970.

Ermarth, Margaret Sittler, *Adam's Fractured Rib,* Fortress Press, Philadelphia, 1970.

Fiorenza, Elisabeth Schussler, *In Memory of Her,* Crossroad, New York, 1983.

Friedan, Betty, *The Feminine Mystique,* Dell Publishing Co., New York, 1963.

Galbraith, John K., "How the Economy Hangs on Her Apron Strings," *Ms.,* May,1974.

Gilligan , Carol, *In a Different Voice,* Harvard University Press, Cambridge and London, 1982.

Good Housekeeping, "What Women Should Know about the Controversy over Breast Surgery," April 1974.

Gornick, Vivian and Barbara K. Moran, *Woman in Sexist Society,* Basic Books, 1971.

Greer, Germaine, *The Female Eunuch,* Bantam Books, New York, 1971.

Hageman, Alice (ed.), *Sexist Religion and Women in the Church,* Association Press, New York, 1974.

Harrison, Michelle, *A Woman In Residence,* Penguin Books, New York, 1982.

Hewitt, Emily C. and Suzanne R. Hiatt, *Women Priests: Yes or No?,* Seabury Press, New York, 1973.

Interpreter's Bible, Abingdon-Cokesbury Press, Nashville, Volumes VII and VIII, 1951.

Janeway, Elizabeth, *Man's World, Woman's Place,* Dell Publishing Co., New York, 1971.

Johnson, Sonia, *From Housewife To Heretic,* Anchor Books, Doubleday, Garden City, New York, 1983.

Kanowitz, Leo, *Women and the Law, The Unfinished Revolution,* University of Mexico Press, 1969.

Major, H. D. A., T.W. Manson, and B. D. Wright, *The Mission and Message of Jesus,* E. P. Dutton & Co., New York, 1946.

Mead, Margaret, *Male and Female,* William Morrow and Co., New York, 1949.

Mill, John Stuart and Harrier Taylor Mill, *Essays on Sex Equality,* University of Chicago Press, Chicago, 1970.

Miller, Jean Baker, *Toward A New Psychology of Women,* Beacon Press, Boston, 1976.

Moltmann-Wendel, Elisabeth, *Liberty, Equality, Sisterhood,* Fortress Press, Philadelphia, 1978.

Montague, Ashley, *The Natural Superiority of Women,* Collier Books, New York, 1971.

Morgan, Robin (ed.), *Sisterhood Is Global,* Anchor Press/Doubleday, Garden City, New York, 1984.

New Catholic Encyclopedia, McGraw-Hill Book Co., New York, 1967.

Paige, Karen E., "Women Learn To Sing the Menstrual Blues," *Psychology Today,* September 1973.

Rogers, Katharine M., *The Troublesome Helpmate: A History of Misogyny in Literature,* University of Washington Press, 1966.

Ruether, Rosemary Radford, "Sexism and the Theology of Liberation," *Christian Century,* December 12, 1973.

_____, (ed.), *Religion and Sexism,* Simon & Schuster, New York, 1974.

Russell, Letty M. (editor), *The Liberating Word,* The Westminster Press, Philadelphia, 1976.

Sayers, Dorothy L., *Are Women Human?,* Inter-Varsity Press, Downers Grove, Illinois, 1971.

Stendhal, Krister, *The Bible and the Role of Women,* Fortress Press, Philadelphia, 1966.

Strack, Paul, and R.E. Billerbeck, *Kommentar zum N.T. aus Talmud und Midrash,* II, 438, quoted in *Interpreter's Bible,* Vol. VIII, pp. 529, 930.

Swidler, Leonard, "Jesus Was a Feminist," *Catholic World,* January 1971.

Trible, Phyllis, *Texts Of Terror,* Fortress Press, Philadelphia, 1978.

_____, *God and the Rhetoric of Sexuality,* Fortress Press, Philadelphia, 1978.

Wahlberg, Rachel Conrad, "K.P., the G.I. and Women," *Christian Century,* June 6, 1973.

_____, "Much Ado About Eve," *Presbyterian Life,* March 15, 1972.

Women, A Questioning of Past and Present, Commission on Church and Society, The American Lutheran Church, Minneapolis, Minn., August 1972.